HM TREASURY

THE GREEN BOOK

Appraisal and Evaluation in Central Government

Treasury Guidance

LONDON: TSO

Contents

	Page
Contents	iv
Preface	v
Chapter 1 Introduction and background	1
Introduction	1
When to use the Green Book	2
Chapter 2 Overview of appraisal and evaluation	3
Introduction	3
The appraisal and evaluation cycle	3
The role of appraisal	3
Process for appraisal and evaluation	4
Presenting the results	6
Managing appraisals and evaluations	7
Frameworks	8
Issues relevant to appraisal and evaluation	9
Chapter 3 Justifying action	11
Introduction	11
Reasons for government intervention	11
Carrying out research	11
Chapter 4 Setting objectives	13
Introduction	13
Objectives, outcomes, outputs and targets	13
Chapter 5 Appraising the options	17
Introduction	17
Creating options	17
Valuing the costs and benefits of options	19
Adjustments to values of costs and benefits	24
Discounting	26
Adjusting for differences in tax between options	28
Introduction to risk and uncertainty	28
Adjusting for bias and risks	29
Assessing uncertainty	32
Preventing and mitigating risks and uncertainty	34
Considering unvalued costs and benefits	34
Chapter 6 Developing and implementing the solution	37
Introduction	37
Selecting the best option	37
Developing the solution	40
Implementation	42
Chapter 7 Evaluation	45
Introduction	45
Evaluation process	45

	Page
Annex 1 Government intervention	51
Introduction	51
Economic efficiency	51
Equity	52
Additionality	52
Regeneration	54
Annex 2 Valuing non-market impacts	57
Introduction	57
Valuing non-market impacts	57
Current research/plausible estimates	59
Valuing environmental impacts	63
Annex 3 Land and buildings	69
Introduction	69
Acquisition and use of property	69
Leases and rents	71
Disposal of property	72
Cost effective land use	72
Annex 4 Risk and uncertainty	79
Introduction	79
Risk management	79
Transferring risk	82
Optimism bias	85
Monte Carlo analysis	87
Irreversible risk	88
The cost of variability in outcomes	88
Annex 5 Distributional impacts	91
Introduction	91
Distributional analysis	91
Analysis of impacts according to relative prosperity	91
Analysis of other distributional impacts	94
Annex 6 Discount rate	97
Introduction	97
Social Time Preference Rate	97
Long term discount rates	98
Exceptions to the discount rate schedule	99
Discount rate tables	100
Glossary	101
Bibliography	107
Index	109

PREFACE

The Government is committed to continuing improvement in the delivery of public services. A major part of this is ensuring that public funds are spent on activities that provide the greatest benefits to society, and that they are spent in the most efficient way.

The Treasury has, for many years, provided guidance to other public sector bodies on how proposals should be appraised, before significant funds are committed – and how past and present activities should be evaluated. This new edition incorporates revised guidance, to encourage a more thorough, long-term and analytically robust approach to appraisal and evaluation. It is relevant to all appraisals and evaluations.

Appraisal, done properly, is not rocket science, but it is crucially important and needs to be carried out carefully. Decisions taken at the appraisal stage affect the whole lifecycle of new policies, programmes and projects. Similarly, the proper evaluation of previous initiatives is essential in avoiding past mistakes and to enable us to learn from experience. The Green Book therefore constitutes binding guidance for departments and executive agencies.

This edition of the Green Book is the first which has been preceded and helped by a consultation. The consultation process has proved invaluable in shaping the final guidance. While the results have shown widespread support for the main changes proposed, the consultation has particularly helped in making the guidance clearer and more closely tailored to users' needs.

Amongst the main changes are the following. First, there is a stronger emphasis on the identification, management and realisation of benefits – in short, focusing on the end in sight, right from the beginning. Secondly, the new edition "unbundles" the discount rate, introducing a rate of 3.5% in real terms, based on social time preference, while taking account of the other factors which were in practice often implicitly bundled up in the old 6% real figure. In particular, the new Green Book includes, for the first time, an explicit adjustment procedure to redress the systematic optimism ("optimism bias") that historically has afflicted the appraisal process. Finally, there is greater emphasis on assessing the differential impacts of proposals on the various groups in our society, where these are likely to be significant.

The Treasury is grateful for the significant contributions to the development of this edition of the Green Book made by many others, working across government and elsewhere. Particular gratitude is due to those who participated in the consultation process and provided such detailed and valuable comments. We hope that the final version reflects the quality of these contributions.

Joe Grice
Chief Economist and Director, Public Services
HM Treasury

INTRODUCTION AND BACKGROUND

INTRODUCTION

1.1 All new policies, programmes[1] and projects, whether revenue, capital or regulatory, should be subject to comprehensive but proportionate assessment, wherever it is practicable, so as best to promote the public interest. The Green Book presents the techniques and issues that should be considered when carrying out assessments.[2]

> The purpose of the Green Book is to ensure that no policy, programme or project is adopted without first having the answer to these questions:
>
> ❑ Are there better ways to achieve this objective?
>
> ❑ Are there better uses for these resources?

1.2 This guidance is designed to promote efficient policy development and resource allocation across government. It does this by informing decision-making, and by improving the alignment of departmental and agency policies, programmes and projects with government priorities and the expectations of the public. The guidance emphasises the need to take account of the wider social costs and benefits of proposals, and the need to ensure the proper use of public resources.

1.3 This is achieved through:

❑ Identifying other possible approaches which may achieve similar results;

❑ Wherever feasible, attributing monetary values to all impacts of any proposed policy, project and programme; and

❑ Performing an assessment of the costs and benefits for relevant options.

> The Green Book describes how the economic, financial, social and environmental assessments of a policy, programme or project should be combined.

1.4 The Green Book is a best practice guide for all central departments and executive agencies, and covers projects of all types and size. It aims to make the appraisal process throughout government more consistent and transparent.

1.5 When more detailed analysis is required, as signposted throughout the Green Book, reference should be made to the technical advice contained in the annexes. These annexes address the needs of specialist technicians and economists by focusing on some of the more involved aspects of appraisal and evaluation. The annexes contain:

---
[1] A programme is defined as a group of related projects
[2] Assessments is the general term used in the Green Book to refer to both appraisals before decisions are made, and evaluations of decisions once made

Chapter 1: The Meaning and Context of Appraisal And Evaluation

❑ Guidance on the conduct of an advanced appraisal; and,

❑ The analytical foundations of the approach contained in the Green Book.

1.6 Departments and agencies should ensure that their own manuals or guidelines are consistent with the principles contained here, providing supplementary guidance on their specific areas.

BOX 1: ACTIVITIES COVERED BY THE GREEN BOOK

Policy and programme development	Decisions on the level and type of services or other actions to be provided, or on the extent of regulation.
New or replacement capital projects	Decisions to undertake a project, its scale and location, timing, and the degree of private sector involvement.
Use or disposal of existing assets	Decisions to sell land, or other assets, replace or relocate facilities or operations, whether to contract out or market test services.
Specification of regulations	Decisions, for example, on standards for health and safety, environment quality, sustainability, or to balance the costs and benefits of regulatory standards and how they can be implemented.
Major procurement decisions	Decisions to purchase the delivery of services, works or goods, usually from private sector suppliers.

WHEN TO USE THE GREEN BOOK

1.7 The Green Book will be useful for:

❑ Anyone required to conduct a basic appraisal or evaluation of a policy, project or programme; and,

❑ People seeking to expand their knowledge in this area.

1.8 This guidance applies:

At the start ... to any analysis used to support a government decision to adopt a new policy, or to initiate, renew, expand or re-orientate programmes or projects, which would result in measurable benefits and/ or costs to the public. This is the *appraisal* part of the process.

And at the finish ... to retrospective analysis of a policy, programme or project at its completion, conclusion or revision. This is the *evaluation* part of the process.

1.9 The ability to judge how effectively government resources have been expended is essential to their strategic long-term management. Planning for this evaluation should be considered at the time of appraisal.

OVERVIEW OF APPRAISAL AND EVALUATION

INTRODUCTION

2.1   This chapter summarises the key stages of appraisal and evaluation. The remaining chapters discuss them in more detail.

THE APPRAISAL AND EVALUATION CYCLE

2.2   Appraisal and evaluation often form stages of a broad policy cycle that some departments and agencies formalise in the acronym ROAMEF (Rationale, Objectives, Appraisal, Monitoring, Evaluation and Feedback). This is shown below:

BOX 2: ROAMEF CYCLE

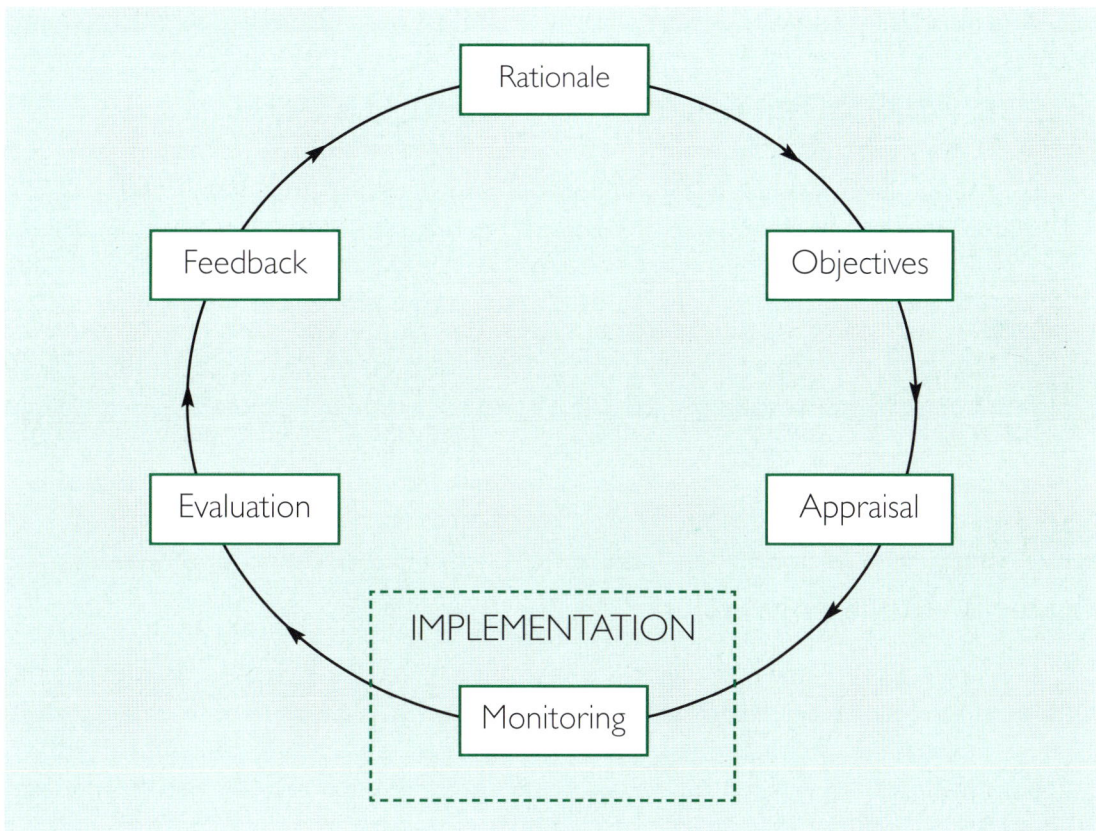

THE ROLE OF APPRAISAL

2.3   Appraisals should provide an assessment of whether a proposal is worthwhile, and clearly communicate conclusions and recommendations. The essential technique is option appraisal, whereby government intervention is validated, objectives are set, and options are created and reviewed, by analysing their costs and benefits. Within this

Chapter 2: Overview of Appraisal And Evaluation

framework, cost-benefit analysis is recommended, as contrasted with cost-effectiveness analysis below, with supplementary techniques to be used for weighing up those costs and benefits that remain unvalued.

> **COST-BENEFIT ANALYSIS**
>
> Analysis which quantifies in monetary terms as many of the costs and benefits of a proposal as feasible, including items for which the market does not provide a satisfactory measure of economic value.
>
> **COST-EFFECTIVENESS ANALYSIS**
>
> Analysis that compares the costs of alternative ways of producing the same or similar outputs.

PROCESS FOR APPRAISAL AND EVALUATION

2.4 Appraisals are often iterated a number of times before their proposals are implemented in full. Therefore the stages set out below may be repeated, and they may not always be followed sequentially. In particular, as options are developed, it will usually be important to review more than once the impact of risks, uncertainties and inherent biases. This helps to avoid spurious accuracy, and to provide a reasonable understanding of whether, in the light of changing circumstances, the proposal is likely to remain good value for money.

2.5 As the stages of an assessment progress, data must be refined to become more specific and accurate. The effort applied at each step should be proportionate to the funds involved, outcomes at stake, and the time available. Accordingly, in the early steps of identifying and appraising options, summary data only is normally required. Later on, before significant funds are committed, the confidence required must increase.

Chapter 3 – Justifying Action

2.6 The first step is to carry out an overview to ensure that two pre-requisites are met: firstly, that there is a clearly identified need; and secondly, that any proposed intervention is likely to be worth the cost. This overview must include an analysis of the negative consequences of intervention, as well as the results of not intervening, both of which must be outweighed to justify action. In many cases, the preliminary step will involve research to set out the scope of the issue to be addressed, and the reasons for intervention.

Chapter 4 – Setting Objectives

2.7 The second step is to set out clearly the desired outcomes and objectives of an intervention in order to identify the full range of options that may be available to deliver them. Targets should be set to help progress towards meeting objectives.

THE GREEN BOOK

Chapter 2: Overview of Appraisal And Evaluation

Chapter 5 – Option Appraisal

2.8 The third step is to carry out an option appraisal. This is often the most significant part of the analysis. Initially a wide range of options should be created and reviewed. This helps to set the parameters of an appropriate solution. A shortlist may then be created to keep the process manageable, by applying the techniques summarised below to high level estimates or summary data. The 'do minimum' option should always be carried forward in the shortlist, to act as a check against more interventionist action.

2.9 Each option is then appraised by establishing a Base Case[1]. This is the best estimate of its costs and benefits. These estimates can then be adjusted by considering different scenarios, or the option's sensitivity to changes can be modelled by changing key variables. More fully, the appraisal may develop as follows:

- Identify and value the costs of each option.
- Identify and value the benefits of each option.
- If required, adjust the valued costs and benefits for:
    - Distributional impacts (the effects of proposals on different sections of society);
    - Relative price movements.
- Adjust for the timing of the incidence of costs and benefits by discounting them, to obtain their present values.
- If necessary, adjust for material differences in tax between options.
- Adjust for risk and optimism to provide the Base Case, and consider the impacts of changes in key variables and of different future scenarios on the Base Case.
- Consider unvalued impacts (both costs and benefits), using weighting and scoring techniques if appropriate.

Chapter 6 – Developing and implementing a solution

2.10 Following option appraisal, decision criteria and judgment should be used to select the best option or options, which should then be refined into a solution. Consultation is important at this stage, regardless of whether it has taken place earlier. Procurement routes should also be considered, including the role of the private sector.

2.11 Issues that may have a material impact on the successful implementation of proposals must be considered during the appraisal stage, before significant funds are committed. This is to ensure that the outcome envisaged in the appraisal is close to what eventually happens.

Chapter 7 – Evaluation

2.12 Evaluation is similar in technique to appraisal, although it obviously uses historic (actual or estimated) rather than forecast data, and takes place after the event. Its main purpose is to ensure that lessons are widely learned, communicated and applied when assessing new proposals.

---

[1] The term 'Base Case' is sometimes used to refer to the 'do minimum' option, but it is not used in this way in the Green Book.

THE GREEN BOOK

PRESENTING THE RESULTS

2.130 The ultimate outcome of any appraisal is a decision whether or not to proceed with a proposal or a particular option. As these decisions will often have far reaching consequences, the presentation of the conclusions and recommendations to decision makers and key stakeholders can be as important as the analysis itself. In all cases, transparency is vital. Presentations and reports should be clear, logical, well founded, and geared towards helping the decision at hand. Summary reports in particular should be drafted in non-technical language wherever possible, but, if it is necessary to use technical terms, they should be explained.

2.14 Reports should provide sufficient evidence to support their conclusions and recommendations. They should provide an easy audit trail for the reader to check calculations, supporting evidence and assumptions. Major costs and benefits should be described, and the values attached to each clearly shown rather than netted off in the presentation of the analysis. This should help to ensure that decision makers understand the assumptions underlying the conclusions of the analysis, and the recommendations put forward. Appraisal reports should contain sufficient information to support the conduct of any later evaluation.

2.15 The results of sensitivity and scenario analyses should also generally be included in presentations and summary reports to decision makers, rather than just single point estimates of expected values. Decision makers need to understand that there are ranges of potential outcomes, and hence to judge the capacity of proposals to withstand future uncertainty.

BOX 3: POSSIBLE OUTPUTS OF AN ECONOMIC APPRAISAL OR EVALUATION

- Business cases (either Preliminary, Outline or Full) consisting of:
    - Strategic Case;
    - Economic Case (or Option Appraisal);
    - Financial Case (or Affordability);
    - Commercial Case;
    - Programme;
    - Project Management Case (or Achievability).
- Regulatory Impact Assessment
- Health Impact Assessment
- Environmental Appraisal
- Health and Safety Impact appraisal
- Consumer Impact Assessment
- Integrated Policy Appraisal (IPA)[2]
- Evaluation and audit reports.

---

[2] The IPA is a policy tool that attempts to cover all aspects of an appraisal. It provides a checklist of questions on issues such as climate change, air quality, landscape, land use, waste, water, biodiversity and noise. Further guidance is available from ODPM, DEFRA and DfT.

Chapter 2: Overview of Appraisal And Evaluation

2.16   Departments and agencies often issue good practice templates for policy and project appraisals and evaluations.[3]

MANAGING APPRAISALS AND EVALUATIONS

2.17   Conducting an assessment can be resource-intensive. Appraisals and evaluations should therefore be carried out collaboratively wherever possible between stakeholders, but lead responsibilities need to be well defined, and accountability for accuracy and thoroughness clearly understood. Carrying out assessments should never be regarded as a specialist activity, and therefore sidelined.

2.18   Departments and agencies should consider how appraisals and evaluations are integrated with decision-making processes and governance structures. To ensure a coordinated approach to conducting assessments, departments and agencies are encouraged to consider:

- Establishing formal evaluation or assessment units, or other centres of technical expertise;
- Formalising access to internal and external auditors. In complex cases, it may be helpful to discuss appraisal methodology with sponsor departments, the Treasury or the National Audit Office;[4]
- Providing incentives for conducting thorough and timely appraisals; and,
- Maintaining an accessible archive.[5]

2.19   For individual assessments, consideration needs to be given at the outset to:

- The availability and cost of financial and specialist resources that may be needed;
- The possible need for quality assurance, for example, by academic experts and service providers;
- How the findings are to be disseminated (e.g. publication of assessments; dissemination via web sites, etc);
- The possibility of deferring a proposal pending further research; and,
- Establishing a project plan for the assessment, setting out key milestones, resources and work streams.

Advice is available on this guidance from:

- Departmental analysts, Public Services Delivery Analysis (PSDA) team in HM Treasury, and a variety of referenced sources on specific issues.
- Training on project and policy assessment is available from a range of sources, including the Civil Service College.

---

[3] For instance, the OGC provides business case templates on its website, which are recommended for use in project appraisals: http://www.ogc.gov.uk

[4] See NAO website: http://www.nao.gov.uk/

[5] See CMPS Knowledge Pools (http://policyhub.gov.uk), and 'Adding It Up' (http://www.addingitup.gov.uk/)

Chapter 2: Overview of Appraisal And Evaluation

FRAMEWORKS

2.20   The frameworks below are particularly relevant to appraisals and evaluations:

- The OGC Gateway Review (mainly for programmes and projects);
- The Regulatory Impact Assessment (mainly for policies involving regulatory impacts); and
- The Centre for Management and Policy Studies (CMPS) Policy Hub.

Office of Government Commerce Gateway Process

2.21   Gateway is a review process for civil procurement projects conducted by the Office of Government Commerce.[6] It examines policies and projects at critical stages in their lifecycle to provide assurance that they can progress successfully to the next stage. Compliance with the Green Book is incorporated into the first and second gateways. Detailed information is available from the OGC website.[7]

Regulatory Impact Assessment

2.22   A regulatory impact assessment (RIA) is a policy tool that assesses the impact, in terms of costs, benefits and risks of any proposed regulation that could affect businesses, charities or the voluntary sector. It is Government policy that all government departments and agencies where they exercise statutory powers and make rules with general effect on others must produce an RIA. They should also produce an RIA for proposed European legislation that will have an effect on businesses, the public sector, charities or the voluntary sector in the UK[8].

2.23   Although the trigger for producing an RIA is that the proposal could affect businesses, charities or the voluntary sector, the RIA itself should cover the full range of economic, social and environmental effects, in line with the Green Book methodology.

The CMPS Policy Hub

2.24   The CMPS Policy Hub[9] aims to improve policy making and delivery, by providing:

- Tailored access to resources and activities from the UK and abroad that help formulate, develop and evaluate policy more efficiently and effectively;
- Innovative examples of improved policy making and delivery;
- Tools to help break down organisational and geographical barriers, and improve collaborative working within and beyond government; and,
- A platform for promoting the highest standards of research and evaluation.

---

[6] Similar processes exist in departments exempt from the Gateway Review Process, for example the Ministry of Defence's 'Smart Acquisition' arrangements. Departments that are exempt should periodically review their monitoring procedures to ensure compliance with the Green Book methodology

[7] OGC website: http://www.ogc.gov.uk/

[8] Guidance is available in Better Policy Making and Regulatory Impact Assessment available from the RIU website: http://www.cabinet-office.gov.uk

[9] See http://www.policyhub.gov.uk

THE GREEN BOOK

Chapter 2: Overview of Appraisal And Evaluation

ISSUES RELEVANT TO APPRAISAL AND EVALUATION

2.25 There is a wide range of generic issues that may need to be considered as part of any assessment. The following list should be checked for relevance to options under appraisal, and used for later evaluations:

- Strategic impact – new proposals can be said to have strategic impacts on organisations if they significantly affect the whole or major part of an organisation over the medium to long term. Proposals should therefore be considered in terms of their potential scale of impact, and how they fit in with the strategy of the organisation(s) they affect.

- Economic rationale – proposals need to be underpinned by sound economic analysis, which should be provided by a cost benefit analysis in an option appraisal. See Chapter 5 in particular.

- Financial arrangements and affordability – proposals need to be affordable, and an affordable financial plan needs to be developed. See Chapter 6.

- Achievability – all proposals should be assessed for their achievability, and recognised programme and project management arrangements set up as necessary. See Chapter 6.

- Commercial and partnering arrangements – proposals need to take account of commercial, partnering and procurement arrangements; what can be delivered in the market; how costs and benefits can be guaranteed through commercial arrangements; how contracts will be managed through to completion. See Chapter 6.

- Regulatory impact – as discussed previously, the impacts of new proposals on businesses, voluntary sector and charities should be assessed. See Chapter 2.

- Legislation – consideration should be given to legislation specific to the case in hand, as well as statutes that affect many proposals, such as the Human Rights Act, or the Data Protection and Freedom of Information Acts.

- Information management and control – The information requirements of proposals, including the data needed for later evaluation, and the supporting IT that may be required. Further guidance is available from the OGC.[10]

- Environmental impacts – The effects on the environment should be considered, including air and water quality, land use, noise pollution, and waste production, recycling and disposal. Further guidance is available from ODPM, Defra and DfT.

- Rural issues – The government is committed to ensuring that all its policies take account of specific rural circumstances. Appraisers should assess whether proposals are likely to have a different impact in rural areas from elsewhere. Further guidance is available from Defra.[11]

- Equality – Impacts on various groups in society should be considered as part of an appraisal. Chapter 5 describes how distributional impacts should be brought into the appraisal process.

---

[10] See http://www.ogc.gov.uk

[11] See http://www.defra.gov.uk

THE GREEN BOOK

Chapter 2: Overview of Appraisal And Evaluation

- ❏ Health – the impacts of proposals on health should be considered, and evaluation made of the impact on health of poverty, deprivation and unemployment, as well as poor housing or workplace conditions. The Department of Health can provide further advice[12], or can be accessed via the policy hub.[13]

- ❏ Health and safety – the health and safety of people at work or arising from work activity may need to be safeguarded. Obviously this is of particular concern in construction. The Health and Safety Commission can provide further advice.[14]

- ❏ Consumer focus – Assessments may need to involve consideration of the cost and quality of goods and services, as well as access to, choice of, and information about them.[15]

- ❏ Regional perspectives – CMPS provides guidance on how regional perspectives are best incorporated into the policy making process.[16]

- ❏ European Union – It will often be important to take account of proposals and activities in other European Union countries, as well as specific legislation and regulations. State aid rules are particularly important to consider, as these prescribe the extent to which government can intervene.[17]

- ❏ Design quality – The design quality of facilities can be important in ensuring that objectives are successfully achieved.[18]

---

[12] See http://www.doh.gov.uk
[13] See http://www.policyhub.gov.uk
[14] See http://www.hse.gov.uk
[15] See http://www.policyhub.gov.uk
[16] See http://www.policyhub.gov.uk
[17] See http://www.dti.gov.uk
[18] See http://www.cabe.org.uk

Justifying Action

Introduction

3.1 Before any possible action by government is contemplated, it is important to identify a clear need which it is in the national interest for government to address. Accordingly, a statement of the rationale for intervention should be developed.

> Key questions for justifying action:
> - Is the rationale for intervention clear?
> - Is it reasonable to assume that intervention will be cost-effective: i.e. that the benefits of intervention will exceed the costs?

Reasons for government intervention

3.2 This underlying rationale is usually founded either in market failure or where there are clear government distributional objectives that need to be met. Market failure refers to where the market has not and cannot of itself be expected to deliver an efficient outcome; the intervention that is contemplated will seek to redress this. Distributional objectives are self-explanatory and are based on equity considerations.

3.3 Government intervention can incur costs and create economic distortions. These must be taken into account to determine whether intervention is warranted. For example, a regulation may be successful in addressing a particular market failure, but might also involve other costs that mean that overall it is not worthwhile.

Carrying out research

3.4 The first step in appraisal is usually to carry out research, to identify the scope of the issues involved and the basis for government action. The research may cover the following:

- The result if nothing changed, or if there was minimal change;
- The market situation (e.g. cause of any market failure, employment levels);
- Current and projected trends and published forecasts (e.g. population, services volume, demand, relative prices and costs);
- Potential beneficiaries (and those who may be disadvantaged);
- Technological developments; and,
- Whether the problem to be addressed changes in scope or magnitude over time e.g., effects can multiply over generations.

Chapter 3: Justifying Action

3.5 Determining the rationale for government intervention is discussed further in Annex 1.

3.6 Box 4 provides an illustrative example to demonstrate the reasoning and evidence that would be required to justify government intervention.

BOX 4: EXAMPLE 'EXPANDING VOCATIONAL TRAINING'

There is evidence that skilled workforces have positive impacts on high-level economic aims, such as productivity and GDP growth. At the same time, there is evidence of a major skills deficiency in the UK, which is reflected in the low numbers holding intermediate level vocational qualifications, compared to Germany and other European countries. There is further evidence that there are three forms of market failure that continue to cause this skills gap:

1. Externalities leading to under-investment in training by employers. Firms are concerned that once trained, an employee will leave the firm before the firm has recouped its investment. Unless training pays off very quickly, firms are therefore reluctant to provide training to their workers.

2. Imperfect information leading to employees being unable to judge the quality of their training or appreciate the benefits. This reduces their willingness to accept lower wages during the training period or to receive any training at all.

3. Credit market imperfections. Training is costly, but individuals expect to obtain higher wages from training. Some individuals may wish to borrow to fund training in the expectation that they will be able to pay back the loan through higher future wages. However, low-paid employees in particular are likely to be credit constrained and unable to obtain loans to pay for training.

These market failures mean that the level of training provided by the market is likely to be inefficiently low from society's point of view. Well-designed government intervention may help to bridge the gap.

Setting Objectives

Introduction

4.1 If an intervention seems worthwhile, then the objectives of the proposed new policy, programme or project need to be stated clearly. This allows the identification of the full range of alternative options which government may adopt.

Objectives, outcomes, outputs, and targets

4.2 Objectives should be stated so that it is clear what proposals are intended to achieve. Objectives may be expressed in general terms so that the range of options to meet them can be considered. The objectives of individual proposals should be consistent with statements of government policy, departmental or agency objectives, departmental Public Service Agreements (PSAs), and wider macro-economic objectives.

4.3 There is usually a hierarchy of outcomes, outputs, and targets that should be clearly set out in an appraisal. Outcomes are the eventual benefits to society that proposals are intended to achieve. Often, objectives will be expressed in terms of the outcomes that are desired. But outcomes sometimes cannot be directly measured, in which case it will often be appropriate to specify outputs, as intermediate steps along the way. Outputs are the results of activities that can be clearly stated or measured and which relate in some way to the outcomes desired.

4.4 Targets can be used to help progress in terms of producing outputs, delivering outcomes, and meeting objectives. Targets should be SMART;

- **S**pecific,
- **M**easurable,
- **A**chievable,
- **R**elevant, and,
- **T**ime-bound.

Chapter 4: Setting Objectives

BOX 5: SETTING OBJECTIVES AND TARGETS

The following questions may help to set suitable objectives and targets:

- ❏ What are we trying to achieve? What are our objectives? What would constitute a successful outcome or set of outcomes?
- ❏ Have similar objectives been set in other contexts that could be adapted?
- ❏ Are our objectives consistent with strategic aims and objectives as set out, for example, in the department's Public Service Agreements (PSA's)?
- ❏ Are our objectives defined to reflect outcomes (e.g., improved health, crime reduction or enhanced sustainable economic growth,) rather than the outputs (e.g. operations, prosecutions or job placements), which will be the focus of particular projects?
- ❏ How might our objectives and outcomes be measured?
- ❏ Are our objectives defined in such a way that progress toward meeting them can be monitored?
- ❏ What factors are critical to success?
- ❏ What SMART targets can we then set? What targets do we need to meet?

BOX 6: EXAMPLES OF OUTPUTS AND OUTCOMES

Policy area	Outputs	Outcomes
Job search / Job matching	Number of job seekers assisted.	Value of extra output, or improvement in efficiency of job search
Development of skills	Number of training places and / or numbers completing training	Value of extra human capital, and / or earnings capacity
Social outputs: Schools; Health centres	Exam results (schools), People treated (health centres).	Improvements in human capital (schools); Measures of health gain (health centres).
Environmental improvement	Hectares of derelict land freed of pollution.	Improvement to the productivity of the land.

THE GREEN BOOK

BOX 7: EXAMPLE 'EXPANDING VOCATIONAL TRAINING'

OVERALL POLICY OBJECTIVE

'To address the major skills deficiency in the UK by increasing training to be reflected in the numbers of people holding vocational qualifications'.

See Box 4 for the rationale for government intervention.

Examples of outcomes, outputs and targets:

Outcomes	Outputs	Targets
A socially optimal level of training	Human capital as a share of GDP	The number of training places that will be provided by a certain date
Higher productivity for both trainees and co-workers	Proportion of workforce with vocational training	Reduction in the percentage drop-out rate by a certain date

Chapter 4: Setting Objectives

APPRAISING THE OPTIONS

5

INTRODUCTION

5.1   The purpose of option appraisal is to help develop a value for money solution that meets the objectives of government action. Creating and reviewing options helps decision-makers understand the potential range of action that they may take.

5.2   The approach set out here explains how options can be created, and values estimated for the Base Case (i.e. the best estimate of the costs and benefits of an option). It goes on to state how the Base Case may be adjusted to account for uncertainty about the future, using sensitivity and scenario analyses, and how to consider non-monetised impacts.

CREATING OPTIONS

5.3   This step involves preparing a list of the range of actions which government could possibly take to achieve the identified objectives. The list should include an option where government takes the minimum amount of action necessary (the 'do minimum option'), so that the reasons for more interventionist actions can be judged.

5.4   The range of options depends on the nature of the objectives. For a major programme, a wide range should be considered before short-listing for detailed appraisal. Both new and current policies, programmes and projects should be included as options. At the early stages, it is usually important to consult widely, either formally or informally, as this is often the best way of creating an appropriate set of options.

5.5   An option may affect, or be affected by, other expenditure across the public sector (for example, where its outputs or costs depend upon another project or the implementation of a related policy perhaps in another department). Where a number of expenditures or activities are linked together and the costs or benefits are mutually dependent, the proposal must be appraised as a whole. However, the contribution of the component parts of each proposal to achieving overall value for money must be taken into account.

BOX 8: CREATING OPTIONS

Establishing a range of options can be challenging. The following actions are suggested:

- ❑ Research existing reports, and consult widely with practitioners and experts, to gather the set of data and information relevant to the objectives and scope of the problem.
- ❑ Analyse the data to understand significant dependencies, priorities, incentives and other drivers.
- ❑ From the research, identify best practice solutions, including international examples if appropriate.
- ❑ Consider the full range of issues likely to affect the objective.
- ❑ Identify the full range of policy instruments or projects that may be used to meet the objectives. This may span different sorts or scales of intervention; regulatory (or deregulatory) solutions may be compared with self-regulation, spending or tax options.

Chapter 5: Appraising the Options

BOX 8: CREATING OPTIONS (contd)

- Develop and consider radical options. These options may not become part of the formal appraisal but can be helpful to test the parameters of feasible solutions. Well-run brainstorming sessions can help to generate such a range of ideas.

BOX 9: EXAMPLES OF OPTIONS

Examples of strategic and operational options include:

- Varying time and scale
- Options to rent, build or purchase
- Changing the combination of capital and recurrent expenditure
- Refurbishing existing facilities or leasing and buying new ones
- Co-operating with other parts of government
- Changing locations or sites
- Provision of the service, such as maintenance, or facility by the private sector
- Co-locating, or sharing facilities with other agencies
- Using IT to improve delivery, as part of wider organisational changes
- Transferring service provision to another body, or improving partnership arrangements
- Varying the balance between outsourcing and providing services (or retaining expertise in-house)
- Engaging the voluntary sector
- Regulation, including private sector self regulation, and voluntary action
- Different standards or compliance procedures for different groups (e.g. large and small businesses)
- Varying quality targets
- Different degrees of compulsion, accreditation, monitoring, and inspection regimes, including voluntary codes, approved codes of practice or government regulation
- Action at a regional, national, or international level (e.g. European wide)
- Better implementation of existing measures or initiatives
- Information campaigns
- Deregulation and non-intervention
- Changes that will be permanent in the foreseeable future, or initiatives with specified time horizons.

Chapter 5: Appraising the Options

Short-listing options

5.6 A shortlist of options may be created, partly to keep the appraisal process manageable, usually at the preliminary stages of a policy appraisal, or during the strategic outline business case stage for a capital investment appraisal. However, there is a risk that the process of short-listing will eliminate the optimal solution before it is given full consideration. Therefore, shortlists should still try to cover a wide range of potential action.

5.7 The shortlist must always include the 'do minimum' option. Reasons behind the rejection of each excluded option should be recorded.

VALUING THE COSTS AND BENEFITS OF OPTIONS

Introduction

5.8 The relevant costs and benefits to government and society of all options should be valued, and the net benefits or costs calculated. The decision maker can then compare the results between options to help select the best. It is important to avoid being spuriously accurate when concluding from, and presenting the results of, data generated by the appraisal. However, the confidence in the data provided by the analysis will need to increase, depending on the importance or scale of the decision at hand (for instance, depending on how much resource will be committed by the decision).

5.9 In this context, relevant costs and benefits are those that can be affected by the decision at hand. Although they will vary depending on the scope of the proposal, some general principles apply. It is useful early on in the appraisal process to consider widely what potential costs and benefits may be relevant.

5.10 Costs and benefits considered should normally be extended to cover the period of the useful lifetime of the assets encompassed by the options under consideration, although, if the appraisal concerns the contractual purchase of outputs and outcomes (e.g. in PFI), the appraisal period may be different.

5.11 Costs and benefits should normally be based on market prices as they usually reflect the best alternative uses that the goods or services could be put to (the opportunity cost). However, market prices may need to be adjusted for tax differences between options.

5.12 Wider social and environmental costs and benefits for which there is no market price also need to be brought into any assessment. They will often be more difficult to assess but are often important and should not be ignored simply because they cannot easily be costed. Annex 2 provides more information on how to take into account the wider impacts of proposals.

5.13 Cashflows and resource costs are also important in an appraisal, as these inform the assessment of the affordability of a proposal. However, they do not provide the opportunity cost and, therefore, cannot be used to understand the wider costs and benefits of proposals. Proposals are also likely to require resource budgets, so that it is clear how they will be funded, and, ex post, accounted for. Chapter 6 provides more information on resource budgets and the other accounting requirements of appraisals.

Chapter 5: Appraising the Options

Estimating costs

5.14 Costs should be expressed in terms of relevant opportunity costs. It is important to explore what opportunities may exist. An example of an opportunity is to use land in a different, more valuable, way than in its current use. Another is the alternative use of an employee's time. Full time equivalent (FTE) costs should be used to estimate the costs of employees' time to the employer[1], and should include pensions, national insurance and allowances, as well as basic salaries.

5.15 Costs of goods and services that have already been incurred and are irrevocable should be ignored in an appraisal. They are 'sunk costs'. What matters are costs about which decisions can still be made. However, this includes the opportunity costs of continuing to tie up resources that have already been paid for.

5.16 It can be useful to distinguish between fixed, variable, semi-variable and step costs:

- Fixed costs remain constant over wide ranges of activity for a specified time period (such as an office building);

- Variable costs vary according to the volume of activity (external training costs, for example, varying with the number of trainees);

- Semi-variable costs include both a fixed and variable component (maintenance is an example, where there is usually a set planned programme, and a responsive regime whose costs vary in proportion to activity, i.e. the number of call-outs); and,

- Semi-fixed, or step costs, are fixed for a given level of activity but they eventually increase by a given amount at some critical point (after telephone call volumes reach a certain level, a new call centre may be required).[2]

5.17 Categorising costs in this way can aid sensitivity analysis, but the categorisation should be used carefully. A cost that is fixed relative to one factor may change with another. More complex modelling may be required to describe how costs change over time and with different variables.

5.18 For substantial proposals, the relevant costs are likely to equate to the full economic cost of providing the associated goods and services, and for these proposals, the full economic cost should be calculated, net of any expected revenues, for each option. The full cost includes direct and indirect costs, and attributable overheads. The full cost of the Base Case, as built up in this way, should also equal the total of the analysis of costs into their fixed, variable, semi-variable and stepped elements. A dual cost analysis of this kind enables opportunity costs to be fully considered, and sensitivity analysis to be conducted later on.

5.19 Appraisals leading to short-term or non-strategic decisions are likely to have a smaller set of relevant costs. The relevant costs are likely to be those that are marginal to the organisation's overall activity.

5.20 Cost estimation can be difficult, depending on the class of costs under consideration. It will normally involve input from accountants, economists and other specialists, depending on the type of appraisal. The appraiser needs to understand and communicate clearly the scope of the appraisal to ensure that specialists provide relevant cost information, whilst ensuring that opportunities have been thoroughly explored.

---

[1] See Annex 2 on the valuation of time to society.

[2] Definitions are taken from Drury (1998)

20 THE GREEN BOOK

5.21 Depreciation and capital charges should not be included in an appraisal of whether or not to purchase the asset that would give rise to them (although for resource budgeting purposes they may be important). Depreciation is an accounting device used to spread the expenditure on a capital asset over its lifetime. Capital charges reflect the opportunity cost of funds tied up in capital assets, once those assets have been purchased. They are used to help test the value for money of retaining an asset. They should not be included in the decision whether or not to purchase the asset in the first place.

5.22 Even where an appraisal covers the full expected period of use of an asset, the asset may still have some residual value, in an alternative use within an organisation, in a second-hand market, or as scrap. These values should be included, and tested for sensitivity, as it may be difficult to estimate the future residual value at the present time.

5.23 Some projects expose the government to contingent liabilities – that is commitments to future expenditure if certain events occur. These should be appraised (and monitored if the proposal goes ahead). One class of contingent liabilities is the cancellation costs for which the government body may be liable if it terminates a contract prematurely. Such liabilities, and the likelihood of their coming about, must be taken into account in appraising the initial proposal. Redundancy payments fall into this category, but as the wider social and economic consequences of these should also be assessed, advice from economists should be sought.[3]

Estimating the value of benefits

5.24 The purpose of valuing benefits is to consider whether an option's benefits are worth its costs, and to allow alternative options to be systematically compared in terms of their net benefits or net costs. The general rule is that benefits should be valued unless it is clearly not practicable to do so. Even if it is not feasible or practicable to value all the benefits of a proposal, it is important to consider valuing the differences between options.

5.25 In principle, appraisals should take account of all benefits to the UK.[4] This means that as well as taking into account the direct effects of interventions, the wider effects on other areas of the economy should also be considered. These effects should be analysed carefully as there may be associated indirect costs, such as environmental costs, which would also need to be included in an appraisal. In all cases, these wider effects should be clearly described and considered.

5.26 Real or estimated market prices provide the first point of reference for the value of benefits. There are a few exceptions where valuing at market prices is not suitable. If the market is dominated by monopoly suppliers, or is significantly distorted by taxes or subsidies, prices will not reflect the opportunity costs and adjustments may be required and specialist economic advice will be needed. An example of this is the effect of EU subsidies on the market for agricultural land.

5.27 The results of previous studies may sometimes be used to estimate the economic value of changes stemming from current programmes or policies. There will be increasing scope for using this 'benefit transfer' method as databases expand, though care must be taken to allow for different circumstances. The characteristics of the consumers or client group for which data exist may differ from those of the proposal under consideration. These factors can limit the extent to which values can be transferred or generalised.

---

[3] Redundancy payments are also examples of transfer payments, which are those for which no good or service is obtained in return. Transfer payments may change the distribution of income or wealth, but do not give rise to direct economic costs.

[4] All impacts (including costs and benefits, both direct and indirect) on non-UK residents and firms should be identified and quantified separately where it is reasonable to do so, and if such impacts might affect the conclusions of the appraisal. Generally, proposals should not proceed if, despite a net benefit overall, there is a net cost to the UK (for instance, after taking into account environmental costs).

Chapter 5: Appraising the Options

5.28 In the absence of an existing robust (i.e. reliable and accurate) monetary valuation of an impact, a decision must be made whether to commission a study, and if so how much resource to devote to the exercise. Annex 2 sets out the key considerations that may govern a decision to commission research.

5.29 Where it is concluded that a research project to determine valuations is not appropriate, a central estimate, together with a maximum and minimum plausible valuation, should be included. These figures should be included in sensitivity analyses to give assurance that benefit valuation is not critical to the decision to be made. A plausible estimate of the value of a benefit or cost can often be drawn out by considering a range of issues which are summarised in Annex 2.

Valuing costs and benefits where there is no market value

5.30 Most appraisals will identify some costs and benefits for which there is no readily available market data. In these cases, a range of techniques can be applied to elicit values, even though they may in some cases be subjective. There will be some impacts, such as environmental, social or health impacts, which have no market price, but are still important enough to value separately.

5.31 Box 10 summarises the main techniques that can be used to elicit these values. Annex 2 describes these techniques in more detail, and provides further information on how they are being applied in practice.

Chapter 5: Appraising the Options

BOX 10: VALUATION TECHNIQUES

Determine whether

| Impacts can be measured and quantified |

AND

| Prices can be determined from market data |

If this cannot be readily done

| Use 'Willingness to Pay' for a benefit | 'willingness to pay'

determined by

| Inferring a price from observing consumer behaviour | 'revealed preference' or a subset of this called 'hedonic pricing'

If this does not provide values, determine whether:

| Willingness to pay can be estimated by asking people what they would be willing to pay for a particular benefit | 'stated preference'

or whether

| In the case of a cost: identifying the amount of compensation consumers would demand in order to accept it | 'willingness to accept'

THE GREEN BOOK 23

Adjustments to values of costs and benefits

5.32 Adjustments will often be required to take account of distributional impacts, and relative price changes to develop the Base Case. As for all adjustments, they should be shown separately, clearly and explicitly in any supporting tables of data.

Distributional analysis

5.33 It is important that the distributional implications of each option are considered during appraisal. This type of analysis enhances the understanding of the fairness of proposals, their social impacts and their scale.

5.34 The impact of a policy, programme or project on an individual's well-being will vary according to his or her income; the rationale being that an extra pound will give more benefit to a person who is deprived than to someone who is well off. In economics, this concept is known as the 'diminishing marginal utility of additional consumption'.

5.35 Other distributional issues may also arise, and should be considered during appraisal. A proposal may have differing impacts according to age, gender, ethnic group, health, skill, or location. These effects should be explicitly stated and quantified wherever feasible. For example, the costs and benefits of a proposal might be broken down according to the ethnic group they accrue to, providing appraisers with a basis for comparison and analysis.

5.36 Generally though, these other distributional issues are largely correlated with income. Therefore, if more in depth analysis is undertaken, it should focus on how the cost and benefits of a proposal are spread across different socio-economic groups.

5.37 For the purposes of project appraisal, relative prosperity may often be best defined by relative income, adjusted for household size, and divided into quantiles (e.g. quintiles or deciles).[5] The equity impact of competing options can be compared by charting the impact each has on different 'quantiles' of the income distribution. Proposals that deliver greater net benefit to households or individuals in lower income quantiles are rated more favourably than those that benefit higher quantiles.

5.38 A more in depth analysis uses distributional weights to adjust explicitly for distributional impacts in the cost-benefit analysis. Benefits accruing to households in a lower quantile would be weighted more heavily than those that accrue to households in higher quantiles. Conversely, costs would be weighted more heavily for households in lower quantiles. Annex 5 provides further guidance in this area.

5.39 A project aiming to improve market efficiency through the correction of market failure needs also to consider equity outcomes. In this case, an explicit adjustment would be particularly helpful as an equity check for the proposal. Similarly, an adjustment is desirable when faced with a decision between competing equity motivated projects, aimed at regenerating areas containing different socio-economic populations.

5.40 Applying an explicit distributional adjustment requires quite detailed information about the affected population. A judgement must be made as to whether the necessary socio-economic information is available at an acceptable cost, given the importance of the proposal and the likely scale of the impact of distributional analysis.

---

[5] The relative prosperity of a household depends on its size and composition as well as income. The varying costs of living of different households can be adjusted for by calculating equivalised income ranges. Further detail is provided in Annex 5.

5.41 Where appraisers decide not to adjust explicitly for distributional impacts, they must provide a justification for this decision. This judgement should be informed by the following considerations:

- The significance of the impact of distributional analysis to the proposal under consideration;
- The ease with which distributional impacts can be measured; and
- The scale of the impact associated with a particular project or proposal.

Adjusting for relative price changes

5.42 The valuation of costs or benefits should be expressed in 'real terms' or 'constant prices' (i.e. at 'today's' general price level), as opposed to 'nominal terms' or 'current prices'.

5.43 If necessary, the effect of expected future inflation in the general price level should be removed by deflating future cash flows by forecast levels of the relevant deflator. Over a long-term period, the Bank of England's annual inflation target[6] is the appropriate measure of prices to use as a general deflator.

5.44 Where particular prices are expected to increase at significantly higher or lower rate than general inflation, this *relative* price change should be calculated. Examples where relative price changes may be material to an appraisal include:

- High technology products, prices for which may be expected to fall in real terms;
- Fuel prices, where the resource supply is scarce; and
- Wages, where productivity growth is expected to lead to wage increases above general inflation.[7]

5.45 It is helpful when anticipating relative price movements, to consider whether the value of a benefit or a cost will rise as incomes increase. The most direct evidence for this is evidence about how, in fact, revealed preference or stated preference valuations of the benefit in question have increased with income over time. In some cases there is reason to expect that the value of a benefit or cost will rise as incomes increase, for example because the good is in fixed supply (such as certain environmental assets), or because the units in which it is measured are such that its utility value can be expected to remain broadly constant, regardless of changes in income. In the absence of definitive data, the rate of increase in the real value of the benefit should be assumed to be positive, and only in unusual circumstances would it exceed the projected rate of increase of per capita real income.[8] Where these assumptions are critical, they should be tested against any specific evidence.

5.46 For other costs and benefits, the factors listed below might be considered in determining whether their value would change by more or less than inflation.

- Scarcity. If a good is exhaustible, its relative price may be expected to rise at a faster rate than general prices, as it becomes increasingly scarce. Against this, developing technologies may enable more of a good to be extracted than initially thought possible.

---

[6] Currently set by the Government at 2.5%.

[7] HM Treasury (2002), 'Trend Growth: Recent Developments and Prospects', projected trend productivity growth of 2%

[8] Any reduction in the discount rate in the longer term should be linked to a proportional decrease in the projected rate of growth of income.

Chapter 5: Appraising the Options

- ❑ Substitutability. Where plenty of substitutes are available, any scarcity impact may be largely offset. Consideration should be given to whether substitutes are likely to develop over time, particularly in the case of exhaustible goods.

- ❑ Non-linearity. Some of the damage resulting from pollutants, for example, will be non-linear. If the quantity of a pollutant changes over time, this non-linearity will affect the rate at which its relative price changes.

- ❑ Increasing competition, or the removal of monopoly powers, would increase the availability of goods and services, and relative prices may be expected to decline.

- ❑ Economies of scale. If the size of the market for a particular good or service increases, then there is a greater potential for economies of scale, and relative prices may then also be expected to reduce.

5.47 Advice on likely relative price movements should be obtained from the appropriate expert bodies and from finance divisions or economists.

DISCOUNTING

5.48 Discounting is a technique used to compare costs and benefits that occur in different time periods. It is a separate concept from inflation, and is based on the principle that, generally, people prefer to receive goods and services now rather than later. This is known as 'time preference'.

5.49 For individuals, time preference can be measured by the real interest rate on money lent or borrowed. Amongst other investments, people invest at fixed, low risk rates, hoping to receive more in the future (net of tax) to compensate for the deferral of consumption now. These real rates of return give some indication of their individual pure time preference rate. Society as a whole, also prefers to receive goods and services sooner rather than later, and to defer costs to future generations. This is known as '*social* time preference'; the 'social time preference rate' (STPR) is the rate at which society values the present compared to the future.

> **The discount rate is used to convert all costs and benefits to 'present values', so that they can be compared. The recommended discount rate is 3.5%. Calculating the present value of the differences between the streams of costs and benefits provides the net present value (NPV) of an option. The NPV is the primary criterion for deciding whether government action can be justified.**

5.50 The mathematical expressions used to calculate discounted present values are set out in the footnote below.[9]

---

[9] Year 0 is the present. Accordingly, the present value, at the middle of year 0, of a payment of £1 made at the middle of year n is given by:

$$D_n = \frac{1}{(1+r)^n}$$

where r is the discount rate and D_n is the discount factor. For example, a payment of £150 at the middle of year 5 has a present value at the middle of year 0 of:

$$£150 \times \frac{1}{(1.035)^n} = £150 \times 0.8420 = £126.30$$

THE GREEN BOOK

5.51 For projects with very long-term impacts, over thirty years, a declining schedule of discount rates should be used rather than the standard discount rate. The schedule of long term discount rates is shown in Annex 6.

5.52 Annex 6 also explains the derivation of the social time preference rate, why the rate declines over time, and the circumstances when exceptions to the standard discount rates are allowed.

5.53 Table 1 shows how the present value of £1,000 declines in future years with a discount rate of 3.5 per cent. More detailed discount rate tables are provided in Annex 6.

TABLE 1: PRESENT VALUES AND DISCOUNT RATE

Time (mid year)	0	1	2	3	4	5	6	7	8	9	10
PV of payment (mid year)	£1,000	£966	£934	£902	£871	£842	£814	£786	£759	£734	£709

Required Rates of Return and Pricing Rules

5.54 Some central government bodies sell goods or services commercially, including to the government itself. These activities may be controlled by requiring prices to be set to provide a required rate of return (RRR) on the capital employed by the activity as a whole. Government policy is generally to set charges for goods and services sold commercially at market prices, and normally to recover full costs for monopoly services, (including the cost of capital as defined in the Treasury Fees and Charges Guide)[10].

---

[10] An update of the Guide is expected to appear on the Treasury website during 2003

Chapter 5: Appraising the Options

> **BOX 11: CALCULATING THE NPV**
>
> Alternative projects, A and B, are both expected to improve the quality of a department's work and reduce staff costs. The Base Case of each is being estimated.
>
> **Option A** requires £10 million in initial capital expenditure to realise benefits of £2.5 million per annum for the following four years (£2 million in reduced staff costs and £0.5 million in quality improvements).
>
> **Option B** requires £5 million in initial capital expenditure to realise benefits of £1.5 million per annum for the following four years (£1 million reduced staff costs and £0.5 million in quality improvements).
>
> *Calculation of Present values*
>
> | Year | 0 | 1 | 2 | 3 | 4 | NPV |
> |---|---|---|---|---|---|---|
> | Discount Factor | 1 | 0.9962 | 0.9335 | 0.9019 | 0.8714 | |
> | **Option A** | | | | | | |
> | Costs/Benefits (£) | -10.00m | 2.50m | 2.50m | 2.50m | 2.50m | |
> | Present Value (£) | -10.00m | 2.42m | 2.33m | 2.25m | 2.18m | **-0.82m** |
> | **Option B** | | | | | | |
> | Costs/Benefits (£) | -5.00m | 1.50m | 1.50m | 1.50m | 1.50m | |
> | Present Value (£) | -5.00m | 1.45m | 1.40m | 1.35m | 1.31m | **0.51m** |
>
> Project B yields a positive net present value of £0.51m compared to -£0.82m for project A and zero for the implicit 'do minimum' alternative. Therefore Project B is preferable.

ADJUST FOR DIFFERENCES IN TAX BETWEEN OPTIONS

5.55 The adjustment of market prices for taxes in appraisal is appropriate where it may make a material difference to the decision. In practice, it is relatively rare that adjustments for taxation are required, because similar tax regimes usually apply to different options. It can also be difficult in practice to estimate costs net of tax. However, where the tax regimes applying to different options vary substantially, this should not be allowed to distort option choice. In such cases it is important to adjust for any differences between options in the incidence of tax arising from different contractual arrangements, such as in-house supply versus buying in, or lease versus purchase. Options attracting different VAT rates, for example, should be compared as if either the same VAT payments, or no payments were made in all cases.

5.56 Where publicly financed options are compared to PFI options, taxation differences should be considered, and adjustments explicitly made if not doing so would materially distort the decision. Specific guidance is available on the Treasury Green Book homepage on how to do this in practice.

INTRODUCTION TO RISK AND UNCERTAINTY

Introduction

5.57 In appraisals, there is always likely to be some difference between what is expected, and what eventually happens, because of biases unwittingly inherent in the appraisal, and risks and uncertainties that materialise. As a

Chapter 5: Appraising the Options

result, risk management strategies should be adopted for the appraisal and implementation of large policies, programmes or projects, but their principles can be applied to smaller proposals.

5.58 Appraisers should calculate an expected value of all risks for each option, and consider how exposed each option is to future uncertainty. Before and during implementation, steps should be taken to prevent and mitigate both risks and uncertainties. It is important to be transparent with sponsors about the potential impact of risks and bias on their proposals.

Risk management

5.59 Risk management is a structured approach to identifying, assessing and controlling risks that emerge during the course of the policy, programme or project lifecycle. Its task is to ensure an organisation makes cost-effective use of a risk process that has a series of well-defined steps to support better decision-making through good understanding of the risks inherent in a proposal and their likely impact. Risk management involves:

- Identifying possible risks in advance and putting mechanisms in place to minimise the likelihood of their materialising with adverse effects;

- Having processes in place to monitor risks, and access to reliable, up-to-date information about risks;

- The right balance of control in place to mitigate the adverse consequences of the risks, if they should materialise; and,

- Decision-making processes supported by a framework of risk analysis and evaluation.

5.60 Annex 4 provides more information on risk management.

ADJUSTING FOR BIAS AND RISKS

Optimism bias

5.61 There is a demonstrated, systematic, tendency for project appraisers to be overly optimistic. This is a worldwide phenomenon that affects both the private and public sectors.[11] Many project parameters are affected by optimism – appraisers tend to overstate benefits, and understate timings and costs, both capital and operational.

5.62 To redress this tendency, appraisers should make explicit adjustments for this bias. These will take the form of increasing estimates of the costs and decreasing, and delaying the receipt of, estimated benefits. Sensitivity analysis should be used to test assumptions about operating costs and expected benefits.

5.63 Adjustments should be empirically based, (e.g. using data from past projects or similar projects elsewhere), and adjusted for the unique characteristics of the project in hand. Cross-departmental guidance for generic project categories is available, and should be used in the absence of more specific evidence.[12] But if departments or agencies have a more robust evidence base for cost overruns and other instances of bias, this evidence should be used in

---

[11] Flyvbjerg, *Underestimating Costs in Public Works Projects – Error or Lie*, APA Journal (2002)

[12] '*Review of Large Public Procurement in the UK*', published in July 2002 (available at: http://www.hm-treasury.gsi.gov.uk/)

Chapter 5: Appraising the Options

preference. When such information is not available, departments are encouraged to collect data to inform their estimates of optimism, and in the meantime use the available data that best fits the case in hand.

5.64 Adjusting for optimism should provide a better estimate, earlier on, of key project parameters. Enforcing these adjustments for optimism bias is designed to complement and encourage, rather than replace, existing good practice, in terms of calculating project specific risk adjustments. They are also designed to encourage more accurate costing. Accordingly, adjustments for optimism may be reduced as more reliable estimates of relevant costs are built up, and project specific risk work is undertaken. Both cost estimates and adjustments for optimism should be independently reviewed before decisions are taken. Annex 4 provides further detail on how to deal with optimism bias.

BOX 12: OPTIMISM BIAS EXAMPLE

> The capital costs of a non-standard civil engineering project are estimated to be £50m NPC in a strategic outline business case (SOBC). No detailed risk analysis work has taken place at this stage, although significant costing work has been undertaken. The project team reports to the project board and applies an optimism bias adjustment of 70%, showing that, for the scope of work required, the total cost may increase by £35 million to £85 million in total. This is based on consultants' evidence, and experience from comparable civil engineering projects at a similar stage in the appraisal process.
>
> As this potential cost is unaffordable, the chief executive requests reductions in the overall scope of the project, and more detailed work for the outline business case stage (OBC). As the project progresses, more costs and specific risks are identified explicitly, despite the reduced scope. For the final business case, the optimism bias adjustment is reduced until there remains only a general contingency of 5% for unspecified risks.
>
> Without applying optimism bias adjustments, a false expectation would have been created that a larger project could be delivered, and at a lower cost.

Valuing risks

5.65 It is good practice to add a risk premium to provide the full expected value of the Base Case. As the previous section explained, in the early stages of an appraisal, this risk premium may be encompassed by a general uplift to a project's net present value, to offset and adjust for undue optimism. But as the appraisal proceeds, more project specific risks will have been identified, thus reducing the need for the more general optimism bias.

5.66 An 'expected value' (EV) provides a single value for the expected impact of all risks. It is calculated by multiplying the likelihood of the risk occurring by the size of the outcome (as monetised), and summing the results for all the risks and outcomes. It is therefore best used when both the likelihood and outcome can be reasonably estimated.

Chapter 5: Appraising the Options

BOX 13: EXAMPLE OF EXPECTED VALUE OF BENEFITS

A new policy was originally expected to generate significant benefits, but following concerns that the original predictions were over optimistic, further risk analysis has confirmed that there is now considerable uncertainty about some of these benefits being realised. Four potential outcomes are now considered possible, with NPVs and probabilities assessed as follows:

	NPV	Probability	Benefits – Expected Values
1	£10 million	0.2	£2 million
2	£20 million	0.4	£8 million
3	£30 million	0.3	£9 million
4	£40 million	0.1	£4 million
Expected value			**£23 million**

The costs of implementation have been more rigorously assessed at between £12-17 million, with an expected value of £15 million.

The expected net benefit is therefore £8 million NPV.

5.67 Decision trees can be useful in this context. They are graphical representations useful in assessing situations in which the probabilities of particular events occurring depend on previous events, and can be used to calculate expected values in these more complex situations. For example, the likelihood of a particular volume of traffic using a road in the future might be dependent on the probability of movements in the oil price. Different scenarios can be analysed in this way.

Chapter 5: Appraising the Options

BOX 14: EXAMPLE – DECISION TREE

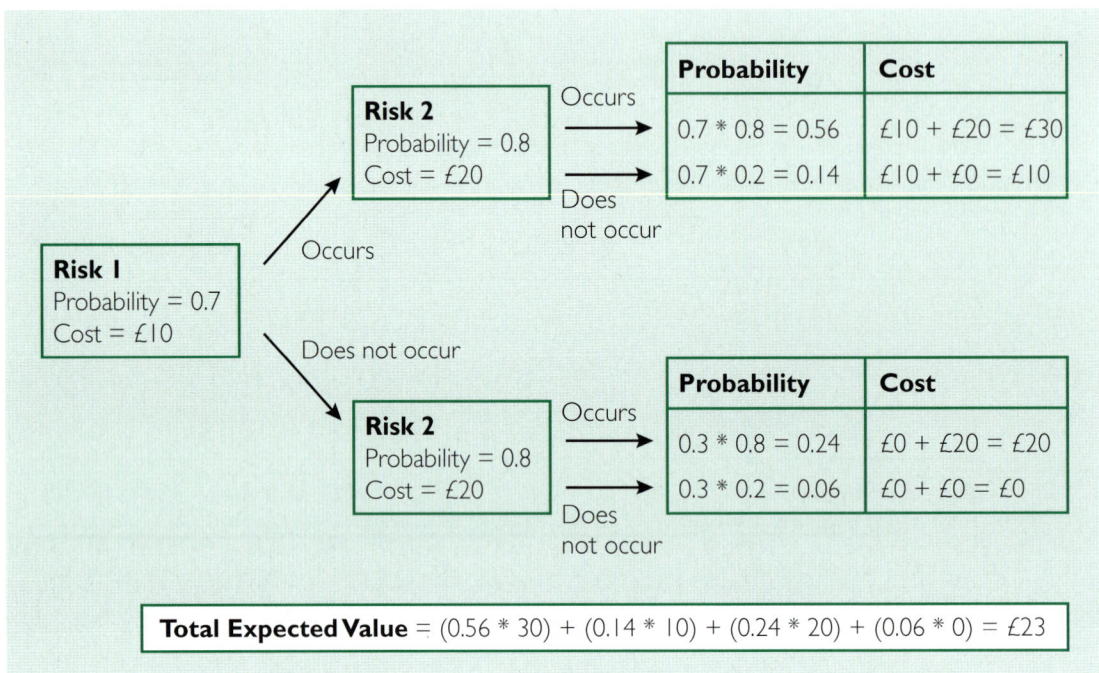

ASSESSING UNCERTAINTY

5.68 An expected value is a useful starting point for understanding the impact of risk between different options. But however well risks are identified and analysed, the future is inherently uncertain. So it is also essential to consider how future uncertainties can affect the choice between options.

Sensitivity analysis

5.69 Sensitivity analysis is fundamental to appraisal. It is used to test the vulnerability of options to unavoidable future uncertainties. Spurious accuracy should be avoided, and it is essential to consider how conclusions may alter, given the likely range of values that key variables may take. Therefore, the need for sensitivity analysis should always be considered, and, in practice, dispensed with only in exceptional cases.

5.70 The calculation of switching values shows by how much a variable would have to fall (if it is a benefit) or rise (if it is a cost) to make it not worth undertaking an option. This should be considered a crucial input into the decision as to whether a proposal should proceed. It therefore needs to be a prominent part of an appraisal.

5.71 Examples of variables that are likely to be both inherently uncertain and fundamental to an appraisal are the growth of real wages, forecast revenues, demand, prices, and assumptions about the transfer of risks. A prior analysis of costs into fixed, step, variable, and semi variable categories can help in understanding the sensitivity of the total costs of proposals.

BOX 15: EXAMPLE OF SENSITIVITY ANALYSIS

A new IT system costs £1million and is expected to yield staff savings of £150,000 per year over a period of 10 years. Discounting at 3.5 per cent the NPV of these costs and benefits is £247,000.

Suppose the estimates of staff savings assumed that the IT system would replace 15 staff with an average cost per person of £10,000. A possible sensitivity test is as follows: what if the IT system replaces only 10 staff? Staff savings would then fall to £100,000 per year and the NPV turns negative (minus £168,000).

Scenarios

5.72 Scenarios are also useful in considering how options may be affected by future uncertainty. Scenarios should be chosen to draw attention to the major technical, economic and political uncertainties upon which the success of a proposal depends. Considering scenarios needs to be proportionate. It may take the form of asking simple 'what if' questions for small and medium sized projects, but extend to creating detailed models of future states of the world for major policies and large programmes. The expected NPV can be calculated for each scenario. It may also be helpful to undertake some sensitivity analysis within a scenario.

BOX 16: EXAMPLE OF SCENARIOS

Box 13 above shows that there is a 20 percent chance that there will be no net benefits (Outcome 1) but a 40 percent chance of net benefits of around £15 million NPV or more (Outcomes 3 and 4). Should it go ahead? Many other considerations then might play, such as whether there are other policies with more certain outcomes? Is it an essential policy area?

Monte Carlo analysis

5.73 Monte Carlo analysis is a risk modelling technique that presents both the range, as well as the expected value, of the collective impact of various risks. It is useful when there are many variables with significant uncertainties. It can be a useful technique but expert advice is required to ensure it is properly applied, especially when risks are not independent of each other. Before undertaking or commissioning such an analysis, it is useful to know how data will be fed into the model, how the results will be presented, and how decisions may be affected by the information generated. An example of Monte Carlo analysis is provided in Annex 4.

PREVENTING AND MITIGATING RISKS AND UNCERTAINTY

5.74 Following the identification and analysis of risks, the generation of an expected value, and an assessment of options' exposure to uncertainty, appraisers need next to look at strategies to prevent and mitigate risks and uncertainties. The following may be adopted:

- Consulting early;
- Avoiding irreversible decisions;
- Carrying out pilot studies;
- Building in flexibility from the start;
- Taking precautionary action;
- Transferring risk through contractual arrangements (insurance being an example);
- Developing less risky options, such as making less use of leading edge technology;
- Reinstating, or developing different options; or,
- Abandoning the project because it is too risky.

5.75 Annex 4 provides more information on what mitigating action might be taken both before and during implementation.

CONSIDERING UNVALUED COSTS AND BENEFITS

5.76 Costs and benefits that have not been valued should also be appraised; they should not be ignored simply because they cannot easily be valued. All costs and benefits must therefore be clearly described in an appraisal, and should be quantified where this is possible and meaningful.

5.77 Research may need to be undertaken to determine the best unit of measurement. Alternative non-monetary measures might be considered most appropriate (See Box 17). For example, one of the benefits arising from a transport improvement is likely to be 'time saved'. These savings must be measured before attaching an aggregate monetary value. In many cases, more than one measure will need to be included to capture the different impacts of the proposal, and the different dimensions of those impacts. For example, there are a number of quantitative indices based on loudness, duration and variability of noise levels. Valuation techniques for use in these circumstances and examples of their application are set out in Annex 2.[13]

---

[13] Reference can be made to the website of the Office of the Deputy Prime Minister: http://www.odpm.gov.uk/.

BOX 17: EXAMPLE OF NON-MONETARY QUANTIFICATION: DESIGN QUALITY INDICATORS

> The Design Quality Indicator (DQI) is a method for assessing the design quality of buildings, which can be used by stakeholders involved in the production and use of buildings, including building users and visitors, and practitioners engaged in the commissioning, design, planning, production and management of the built environment.
>
> The DQI can be used at any stage in the development process, from setting the brief, evaluating design proposals, during construction, and when a building is complete, to set and check that the intentions for the quality of the building are being met.[14]

5.78 The most common technique used to compare both unvalued costs and benefits is weighting and scoring (sometimes called multi-criteria analysis). The basic approach to weighting and scoring involves assigning weights to criteria, and then scoring options in terms of how well they perform against those weighted criteria. The weighted scores are then summed, and these sums can be used to rank options. An even simpler method is to list the required performance criteria (sometimes called 'critical success factors'), and assess options in terms of whether they meet them or not.

5.79 In practice, the weight to give to factors that are thought to be important by key players cannot be decided by 'experts'. They inevitably incorporate the judgments of stakeholders and decision makers. The risk that they are weighted towards acceptance of more expensive solutions by those who would enjoy the potential benefits should be tempered by at least one stakeholder representing the opportunities that an expensive solution would be foregone elsewhere. There are other pitfalls to avoid in carrying out this type of analysis, and reference should be made to guidance on multi-criteria analysis.[15]

---

[14] For further information refer to http://dqi.org.uk, http://www.cic.org.uk, or http://www.cabe.org.uk

[15] An introduction to multi-criteria decision analysis-weighting and scoring – is given in *Multi-Criteria Analysis*. A manual available from the ODPM website: http://www.odpm.gov.uk (see DTLR archive)

Chapter 5: Appraising the Options

BOX 18: EXAMPLE – WEIGHTING AND SCORING

In order to support the introduction of a new training programme, and other departmental objectives, a new IT system is required. A budget of £900,000 is available. The project team discussed with managers and staff the relative importance of the unvalued benefits required of the new system, and submitted proposed weights to be used in the evaluation to the project board, which approved them. For the purposes of this example, only two of the benefits are shown.

Benefit	Weight attached
Ability to provide SMART management information	10
User friendliness – ease of data entry and screen management	20

Three options, based on different systems, were being appraised. Each member of the project user group provided a score for the user friendliness of the systems. Managers provided scores for the management information the systems provided. These were averaged to provide the following scores:

	Management Information	User friendliness
Risk and optimism adjusted costs:		
Option A £1,000,000	6	8
Option B £800,000	6	5
Option C £600,000	8	4

The weighted score of each option was therefore:

Option A	220
Option B	160
Option C	160

Option A has the highest score, but costs 25% more than option B, and 67% more than Option C, and is 11% greater than the available budget. Should it be accepted?

On a further analysis, a conservative estimate was that the time saving for staff from the user friendliness of the system, where Option A scores most highly, would come near to, or equal, the 67% extra cost over Option C. On the other hand, the additional management information – Option C's strong point – could not be substantiated as leading to general improvements in performance. Option A also retained the flexibility for additional management information tools, which could be considered later as part of a separate, smaller business case.

On this basis, the Finance Director decided to fund Option A.

DEVELOPING AND IMPLEMENTING THE SOLUTION

INTRODUCTION

6.1 Following the identification and description of all costs, benefits and risks, their valuation where feasible, and their testing through sensitivity and scenario analysis, the best option should be selected. Transparency is important at this stage, so that it is clear on what basis decisions are taken. Judgement over and above the component parts of the analysis is always called for in making decisions, but the following guidelines should be applied.

6.2 Once an option has been selected, it will need to be refined into a solution. Consultation is important at this stage. Further consideration will need to be given to the implementation of the proposal, including the involvement of the private sector, procurement options and processes, and the programme and project management arrangements that may be required.

SELECTING THE BEST OPTION

Decision guidelines

6.3 If a full cost benefit analysis has been undertaken, the best option is likely to be the one with the highest risk adjusted net present value. To the extent that all costs, benefits and risks have been robustly valued, this guideline can be applied with more certainty. In cost effectiveness analysis, the option with the lowest net present cost should be the best, again assuming that the cost estimates are as accurate and reliable as possible.

6.4 If there is a budget ceiling, then the combination of proposals should be chosen that maximises the value of benefits. The ratio of the net present value to the expenditure falling within the constraint can be a useful guide to developing the best combination of proposals.

BOX 19: EXAMPLE – PROJECT CHOICE

Consider the investment costs and expected net benefits of the following proposals:

	£million Initial investment	Expected net benefit (NPV)
A	10	4
B	6	3
C	4	3

(a) If the budget were constrained to £10 million, proposals B and C would achieve the highest return, rather than proposal A, even though proposal A has the highest individual NPV.

(b) If it is possible that elements of proposals A, B and C could be combined, within the constraint, to produce a significantly higher return, this should be investigated.

Chapter 6: Developing and Implementing the Solution

6.5 Other decision criteria can be used to help select options where risk is an important consideration. The 'maximin-return' option is the most important to consider. It is the most risk averse option, as it is the option that provides the least bad outcome if the worst possible conditions prevail.

BOX 20: EXAMPLE – MAXIMIN RETURN

Two government services are being considered, which are mutually exclusive. Their NPVs under different market conditions are shown below:

	Low demand (£)	Expected value (£)	High demand (£)
Service A	1,000,000	1,200,000	1,600,000
Service B	100,000	1,250,000	2,000,000

The maximin criteria points to Service A, as it provides the highest value in the worst market conditions.

6.6 In practice, other factors will also affect the selection of the best option, in particular the consideration of unvalued costs and benefits. Weighting and scoring techniques are useful in comparing different options in terms of the same criteria. However, as scores are not expressed in monetary terms, judgment is then required to compare the results of weighting and scoring with the cost benefit or cost effectiveness analysis. The two analyses should complement each other, and may indicate that further analysis is required before a decision can be reached. Annex 2 provides further information on how weighting and scoring can be brought into the decision making process. Fully involving stakeholders is very important in making judgments between monetised and non-monetised effects.

6.7 There is always a value imputed by decisions to proceed, and this value should always be clearly identified and analysed.

BOX 21: EXAMPLE – SELECTING THE BEST OPTION

Two lead options are being considered, with net present costs of £1 million and £3 million respectively, after taking into account valued benefits. To select the £3 million option, a decision maker would need to judge that the unvalued benefits of the project must be worth at least £2 million.

He or she needs to judge whether this is reasonable. Several considerations could help inform this judgment. Are there any measures of the unvalued benefits that could be used to derive unit values, which could help assess whether the £2 million is in fact worthwhile? Have values for this kind of benefit been estimated in other studies? Or are there better opportunities elsewhere for using the £2 million? What do the stakeholders think? And importantly, what do the stakeholders representing the opportunity of using the £2 million elsewhere think?

Chapter 6: Developing and Implementing the Solution

6.8 The 'pay back period'[1] is sometimes put forward as a decision criterion. But payback ignores the differences in values over time, and the wider impacts of proposals. These drawbacks mean it should not generally be used as a decision criterion.

6.9 Similarly, the 'internal rate of return'[2] (IRR) should be avoided as the decision criterion. Whilst it is very similar to NPV as a criterion, there are some circumstances in which it will provide different, and incorrect, answers. For instance, IRR can rank projects that are mutually exclusive differently from NPV.

Affordability, funding, and cashflows

6.10 The affordability of options should always be considered when developing and selecting options. In addition to the analysis of economic costs and benefits, appraisals usually need three major financial statements, at least for the lead options:

- A *budget* statement. This should be based on resource accounting and budgeting (RAB) principles, and show the resource costs over the lifetime of the proposal. For strategic initiatives, the budget will often comprise the forecast RAB financial statements of a whole organisation over a number of years.

- A *cashflow* statement. This should show the additional cash that will be spent on the lead option if it goes ahead.

- A *funding* statement. This should show which internal departments, partners and external organisations would provide the resources (and in some cases cash) required.

6.11 Contingency arrangements should also be developed to ensure there is sufficient financial cover for risks and uncertainties.

BOX 22: EXAMPLE – DIFFERENCES BETWEEN COSTS

A project affecting 1000 existing employees in Department A involves a new project team of 10 additional people, plus an informal 'secondment' from Department B of another 15 people for six months each. Department B has also agreed to fund half of the additional cashflows expected to be incurred.

- The additional *cashflows* involve the costs of employing the additional 10 people.

- The *economic cost* of the proposal includes the cashflows of the additional 10 people, the costs to the 1000 employees affected in Department A (for instance, reflecting the cost of their time), and the costs of the 15 staff transferred.

- A brief *funding statement* could show that Department B is providing half the additional cashflows expected to be incurred.

- Both departments will need to consider how the transfers affect their staff resource profiles, and potentially other internal budgets.

---

[1] A pay back period is the number of years before a project breaks even; when total (discounted or undiscounted) benefits (net of on-going costs) equal capital costs. This technique ignores all benefits and costs arising after the break-even date and is likely to distort project choice.

[2] The internal rate of return (IRR) is the discount rate that would give a proposal a present value of zero. IRR can be used to rank proposals. In the private sector, hurdle IRRs are often used to test whether a proposal should go ahead. The riskier the project is, the higher the hurdle IRR.

Chapter 6: Developing and Implementing the Solution

DEVELOPING THE SOLUTION

Introduction

6.12 The best option is likely to require further refinement before a solution emerges. Options are rarely completely mutually exclusive, so it is useful to review the other options to see if their good parts can be grafted onto the leading option.

Consultation

6.13 Consultation with external experts and with those affected is very important at this stage, whether or not formal or informal consultation has taken place earlier on.

6.14 Consultation on projects will usually be on one or two lead proposals; whereas consultation on policy and programme proposals that have more widespread effects should usually be undertaken both earlier, and on a wide range of options and alternatives.

6.15 Analysis of who is affected by a proposal, undertaken as part of the appraisal, may be very useful in determining who should be consulted, and also in considering the details of implementation. Attention should be drawn to the key assumptions, options and implementation issues. Consultation exercises should be drawn up in line with the following best practice guidelines:[3]

- Use the most appropriate approach. Written consultation may not the best way to canvass views on a policy or project option. Methods include meetings with interested parties and user surveys.
- Consultation should be easy to respond to (e.g., by electronic means).
- Check if statutory obligations apply.
- Allow sufficient time; consultation should be built into the planning process at the start.
- Be clear about who is being consulted, about what, in what time-scale, for what purpose.
- Consider joining up with other consultations, for instance in other government departments.
- Consultation documents should be clear, concise and focused.
- Ensure that the process reaches the target audience.
- Ensure that people are told the results, and the reasons for decisions taken.

Involving the private sector

6.16 The extent of involvement of the private sector can vary from minor elements of a proposal being contracted-out through to full privatisation, with various forms of contracting, outsourcing and PPPs (including PFI) in between. Public bodies need to consider carefully which procurement route is likely to be most effective. In some cases, the appropriate balance between public or private sector provision will be clear. In others, the best solution must be identified across a range of public, private and partnership options.

---

[3] For further information on carrying out consultation exercises, refer to the Cabinet Office (http://www.cabinet-office.gov.uk/)

Chapter 6: Developing and Implementing the Solution

BOX 23: CONSIDERING PRIVATE SECTOR PROVISION

Private sector provision may be more likely to provide a better solution where the scope for the following is greatest:

- Innovation to reduce costs or to improve observable outcomes;
- Generating additional revenue flows by sales to third parties;
- Reduction in risk of cost overrun or benefit shortfall;
- A contractor is able to exploit economies of scale in the provision of services (e.g. IT support or facilities maintenance);
- Savings in whole life costs and/ or for improved outcomes through effective design (e.g.: where a broad range of services may be provided in association with an asset, or when many inputs must be integrated in delivering a service, or where whole life and operating costs are importantly determined by good design);
- Clear specification of quality standards in absolute terms or in terms of client satisfaction;
- Ability of private sector to control discrete elements of the project without excessive oversight or interference; or,
- Clear boundaries and interfaces between public and private sectors.

Provision by the private sector may be less appropriate where:

- Risks which threaten the viability of a project are outside the control of the contractor (and these risks cannot be separated contractually from the project);
- The predominant risks are ones where the public sector has the comparative advantage in managing them;
- A large degree of discretion is required in determining the quality of services, and quality is not observable; or,
- Bidding costs are large in proportion to the value of the project (although there may be means of reducing these costs).

Commercial agreements

6.17 Appraisals are generally made up of estimates that are forecast some time in advance of either the projected costs being incurred or benefits being realised. Any estimate made well in advance may or may not prove to be correct once a project has been implemented. The less well developed an appraisal, the greater the variability there is likely to be between the estimated value attached to a cost or benefit and the outturn.

6.18 By transferring risk away from the public sector in different ways, different procurement options provide procuring authorities with choices about how they might manage and mitigate certain risks around estimated costs and benefits. For example, typically PFI contracts transfer to the PFI partner the risk that capital costs will exceed estimates made by the procuring authority in a way that some conventional contracts may not. Equally, a payment

Chapter 6: Developing and Implementing the Solution

mechanism that calibrates payments made under a contract with the delivery of well-defined benefits provides procuring authorities with a way of ensuring that certain costs are incurred only if certain benefits are delivered.

6.19 The level of confidence that public bodies can have that estimated costs and benefits will be similar to eventual outturn will depend on:

❑   The length of time between the cost or benefit estimate being made and the date of contract award; and,

❑   The procurement option chosen.

6.20 In relation to the latter, for example, costs which are fixed under contract and which become payable against measured milestones of physical progress in construction will have a higher probability of being incurred than costs which, although fixed under contract, are only payable to the extent that defined benefits, outcomes or contractual outputs associated with the contract are delivered. Comparisons between various procurement options need to take account of the impact that different contractual terms have on the likelihood that, in fact, certain costs will be incurred and benefits realised at the level estimated by the procuring body.

Procurement processes

6.21 OGC provides detailed guidance on the procurement options that are available, and how to conduct the relevant procurement process.[4] If the private sector is involved, proposals should be fully developed before tenders are invited. Where implementation will be by procurement, there are extensive requirements that need to be met under European Commission Directives and also under regulations within the United Kingdom.

6.22 Often, these impose requirements over and above those stipulated by the Green Book, and must be complied with at all stages. Specialist advice can be sought from either the procurement unit within a department or agency or from OGC[5], and from Partnerships UK[6] for PPP and PFI projects. The OGC also provides guidance on partnering arrangements.

IMPLEMENTATION

6.23 Implementation[7] plans should be sufficiently complete to enable decisions to be taken on whether or not to proceed. So that evaluations can be completed satisfactorily later on, it is important that during implementation, performance is tracked and measured, and data captured for later analysis.

Programme and project management

6.24 Economically justifiable and financially affordable proposals are of no value if realistically they cannot be implemented. The implementation of proposals must be considered as part of the appraisal process, enough to

---

[4] See OGC website: http://www.ogc.gov.uk/

[5] Information on European practice is available from http://europa.eu.int and from OGC http://www.ogc.gov.uk/

[6] See http://www.partnershipsuk.org.uk/

[7] In this context, 'implementation' refers to those activities that are required during the period after appraisal to put in place a policy, or complete a programme or project.

Chapter 6: Developing and Implementing the Solution

ensure at least that proposals are viable, risks are manageable, and that benefits can be realised, before significant funds are committed. These aspects of appraisal develop iteratively as with the analysis of costs and benefits.

6.25 Programme management is a structured framework for defining and implementing change within an organisation. It provides a framework for implementing business strategies and initiatives through the management of a portfolio of projects that give organisations the capability to achieve benefits that are of strategic importance. All large programmes should have recognised programme management methodologies.

6.26 There should be an agreed approach to the management of projects, using recognised project management methodologies, such as PRINCE2.[8] Typically, this will involve identifying tasks and responsibilities and deadlines for completing them, and producing baseline schedules of milestones and activities (often in the form of Gantt charts). Progress against the base schedule should be reported on a regular basis. Guidance on project management is available from OGC.[9] Specific guidance is available on the management of construction projects.[10]

Performance management and measurement

6.27 Performance management concerns tracking the success of a policy, programme or project in achieving its objectives and in securing the expected benefits. For appraisal and evaluation purposes, it involves the systematic collection of data relating to the financial management and outcomes of the policy, programme or project during implementation.

6.28 This provides an essential source of information, indicating the extent to which objectives are being achieved, giving an early warning of potential problems, and of the possible need to adapt the policy, programme or project to ensure success. Monitoring also provides information for the evaluation stage. To be fully effective, plans for monitoring must form part of the initial planning of a policy, programme or project.

6.29 Effective performance measurement and monitoring means tracking all categories of benefit and ensuring that:

- Projects have defined target benefits and outputs;
- Ownership of the delivery of benefits remains with the programme manager;
- Outputs of a project or policy remain consistent with changing government objectives;
- Targets and achieved benefits are measured, reported and communicated;
- Costs are closely monitored and managed; and,
- Forecast costs and benefits are frequently reviewed.

6.30 A monitoring system should establish:

- Whether management data is actually measuring what it purports to measure; and,
- Put in place sufficient controls to ensure that the data is accurate.

---

[8] See OGC website: http://www.ogc.gov.uk/

[9] See http://www.ogc.gov.uk

[10] OGC and HM Treasury have produced a series of ten procurement guides for construction projects. These are fully endorsed by the National Audit Office. http://www.property.gov.uk/

Financial reporting

6.31 Regular financial reporting on policies, programmes and projects should be performed. Reports may be integrated into the normal financial reporting cycle of an organisation, issued separately, or possibly combined with the reporting of progress against plan, benefits, and risks.

6.32 Finance reports are likely to show expenditure to date, forecasts for the year, and variances against budgets. In large complex projects, the financial reporting is likely to integrate with contract management, with contractors providing regular 'Work In Progress' statements.

Benefits realisation management

6.33 Benefits realisation management is the identification of potential benefits, their planning, modelling and tracking, the assignment of responsibilities and authorities and their actual realisation. In many cases, benefits realisation management should be carried out as a duty separate from day to day project management.

6.34 Benefits fall into four main categories, which are described below.

BOX 24: BENEFIT CATEGORIES

Benefit		Example
Financial	Quantitative	Operating cost reduction, revenue increase
Non-financial	Quantitative	Number of customer complaints, reduction in road accidents, percentage of government departments on-line
Non-financial	Qualitative	Staff skills, staff morale
Outcomes	Quantitative and qualitative	Improved standards of healthcare

6.35 It is also useful to identify financial savings that release cash for other uses.

Contract management

6.36 When contracts have been let, it will be important to ensure that the respective roles and responsibilities set out in the contract are fully understood and fulfilled to the contracted standard. The likelihood of the benefits being realised will be affected by the contractual terms, and any incentives built in to the contract. Where contracted standards are not fulfilled, the contracting public body should apply mechanisms established in the contract to rectify any under-performance. Guidance is available from OGC on dispute resolution.[11]

---

[11] See http://www.ogc.gov.uk/

EVALUATION

INTRODUCTION

7.1 When any policy, programme or project is completed or has advanced to a pre-determined degree, it should undergo a comprehensive evaluation. Major or on-going programmes, involving a series of smaller capital projects, must also be subject to ex post evaluations.

7.2 Evaluation examines the outturn of a policy, programme or project against what was expected, and is designed to ensure that the lessons learned are fed back into the decision-making process. This ensures government action is continually refined to reflect what best achieves objectives and promotes the public interest.

7.3 Evaluation comprises a robust analysis, conducted in the same manner as an economic appraisal, and to which almost identical procedures apply. It focuses on conducting a cost benefit analysis, in the knowledge of what actually occurred rather than what is forecast to happen.

7.4 In preparing for an evaluation, it is usually helpful to start with an outline plan, setting out the general boundaries of the proposed evaluation, including:

- Questions which it seeks to answer;
- Staff and other resources available;
- Provisional timing and cost; and
- Who should be consulted.

EVALUATION PROCESS

7.5 The evaluation itself would normally follow this sequence:

1. Establish exactly what is to be evaluated and how past outturns can be measured.
2. Choose alternative states of the world and/or alternative management decisions as counterfactuals.
3. Compare the outturn with the target outturn, and with the effects of the chosen alternative states of the world and/or management decisions.
4. Present the results and recommendations.
5. Disseminate and use the results and recommendations.

Chapter 7: Evaluation

> Evaluation requires management initiative (sometimes political commitment) and intensive monitoring. The thoroughness of an evaluation should depend upon the scale of the impact of a policy, programme or project, and to some extent on the level of public interest. There may be a high level of media interest around a project which has required a significant degree of expenditure, or one which is highly complex, novel, or represents a pilot for future large scale programmes. Evaluation reports should be widely disseminated and published, where appropriate, to contribute to the knowledge base upon which future decisions will be taken.

Establish what is to be evaluated

7.6 The activity to be evaluated needs to be clearly specified. The evaluation might be of a project, programme or policy, particular aspects of the activity, or of key common issues affecting a number of activities. It might also be a pilot designed especially for evaluation.

7.7 Objectives, outcomes and outputs should be defined and quantified as precisely as possible for use in step three below.[1] It is important to distinguish between the objectives and outcomes, and the outputs and targets.

7.8 The availability of output and performance measures and targets, and other monitoring data, and how they relate to the objectives should be reviewed. If this information is inadequate, consideration should be given to the collection of additional data, although ideally, data needs would have been considered at the outset of the project.

Alternative States / Management Decisions

7.9 The definition of exactly what needs to be compared with what needs to be clearly stated. The outturn of any complex activity will never be exactly as projected in advance. However, the reasons for the outturn being better or worse than expected may be attributable to the 'state of the world', or to actions of the responsible body. These might include the management of the project, forecasting assumptions, or the inherent design of the policy.

Compare the Outturn with Targets

7.10 As discussed earlier, the technical methodologies used for appraisal and evaluation are similar. Each should identify and measure, where possible, both the direct and indirect benefits of the policy, programme or project. The main difference is that evaluation tends to be based on actual data, and appraisal on forecasts and projections.

7.11 The evaluation should include the following:

- ❑ An assessment, quantified where possible, of what happened;
- ❑ A comparison with the target outturn; and
- ❑ A comparative assessment of one or more counterfactuals (i.e. alternative outturns given different states of the world, or different management decisions).

---

[1] The objectives, outcomes and outputs of a policy, programme or project should have been identified and documented during appraisal. See Chapter 4 for more detail.

Chapter 7: Evaluation

7.12 Where possible the comparative assessment should include a 'control group', to whom the activity was not applied.

7.13 It is usual to take as a benchmark for comparison, what would have happened if the activity under consideration had not been implemented. It is also useful to consider the consequences of implementing one or more of the alternatives considered during appraisal. Occasionally it may be appropriate to consider an option that was not originally appraised, as long as it was feasible at the time of implementation.

7.14 The evaluation should assess the success of the project, programme or policy in achieving its objectives, and also how this achievement has contributed to the wider outcomes. If the objectives were not achieved, the evaluation should establish why that was the case.

Presentation of results and recommendations

7.15 The results of an evaluation should summarise:

- Why the outturn differed from that foreseen in the appraisal;
- How effective the activity was in achieving its objectives, and why;
- The cost effectiveness of the activity; and
- What the results imply for future management or policy decisions.

7.16 The results obtained should generally lead to recommendations for the future. These may include, for example, changes in procurement practice, delivery, or the continuation, modification, or replacement of a programme.

Disseminate the results and recommendations

7.17 The results and recommendations from evaluation should feed into future decision making. The methods used to achieve this will generally require senior management endorsement. Efforts should be made to disseminate the results widely, and, for this purpose, it may be helpful to use summaries of the main points, and reports which synthesise the results from a number of evaluations with common features.

7.18 Evaluation reports and the research that informs them should be placed in the public domain unless there are good reasons, in terms of security or commercial confidentiality, for not doing so.

Comparison of Appraisal and Evaluation

7.19 Box 25 sets out the differences between undertaking an assessment at the outset, in support of government intervention – appraisal – and undertaking an assessment to evaluate how successful such action has been – evaluation.

Chapter 7: Evaluation

BOX 25: COMPARISON OF APPRAISAL AND EVALUATION

	Appraisal	**Evaluation**
Aim	Ex ante assessment of whether action is worthwhile and impacts	Ex post assessment of whether action was worthwhile and impacts
Use of Output	Project procurement, policy and programme design	Feedback for: (a) future procurement, project management, (b) wider policy debate, and (c) future programme management.
Application	Projects, policies and programmes	Projects, policies and programmes
Timing	Always prior to implementation	❑ During implementation ('formative') ❑ After implementation ('summative')
Data	Forecasted	Historic and current, estimated and actual. Estimates of counterfactuals
Method	Comparison of options against 'do nothing' option Estimated assessment of risk	Comparison of results against 'do nothing' option Comparison of actual outturns against target outturns/ alternative outturns Assessment of risks that did or did not materialise
Analytical Techniques	Cost Benefit/ Effectiveness Analysis Discounted cash flow analysis Multi-criteria analysis Other statistical analysis	Cost Benefit/ Effectiveness Analysis Discounted cash flow analysis Multi-criteria analysis Other statistical analysis – e.g.: analysis of performance indicators
Decision Criteria	Comparison of NPV, NPC for different options Non quantifiable factors may be included if quantification impossible	Consideration of whether correct criteria were used
Audit and Enforcement	Public Accounts Committee (PAC), NAO, HMT, OGC Gateways 0, 1 Departmental arrangements	PAC, NAO, HMT, OGC Gateway 5, Departmental arrangements

THE GREEN BOOK

BOX 26: EXAMPLE 'EXPANDING VOCATIONAL TRAINING' - QUESTIONS FOR EVALUATION:

- To what extent did the anticipated costs and benefits match the actual outcome ('benefits realisation')?

- In the light of experience with the target group of trainees, would better results have been achieved if this group had been more tightly defined, e.g. the alternative option of focusing purely on low or unskilled workers?

- Has any new information about the impact of vocational training come to light since the policy was implemented? (i.e. how effective is it in meeting objectives)?

- Were the risks assumed for completion of the training course justified or did they understate/exaggerate the true risk?

- Control group – how does the productivity of those individuals who undertook training compare to the productivity of workers of similar skill who were not offered training?

GOVERNMENT INTERVENTION

ANNEX 1

INTRODUCTION

1   This Annex discusses the rationale for government intervention, whether via a new or changed policy, a programme or a project. It is essentially twofold:

- ❑ The achievement of economic objectives by addressing inefficiencies in the operation of markets and institutions; and,

- ❑ The achievement of an equity objective, such as local or regional regeneration.

ECONOMIC EFFICIENCY

2   Economic efficiency is achieved when nobody can be made better off without someone else being made worse off. Such efficiency enhances prosperity by ensuring that resources are allocated and used in the most productive manner possible. One potential cause of inefficiency is where circumstances mean that the private returns which an individual or firm receives from carrying out a particular action differ from the returns to society as a whole. Market failure is a description of a situation where, for one reason or other, the market mechanism alone cannot achieve economic efficiency. This can occur for a number of reasons, which are briefly discussed below.

Public Goods

3   The market may have difficulty supplying and allocating certain types of products and services, such as 'public goods'. Public goods are those that are 'non-rival' or 'non-excludable' when used or consumed.

- ❑ 'Non-rival' means that the consumption of the good by one person does not prevent someone else using or consuming that good. Clean air is an example of a non-rival good.

- ❑ 'Non-excludable' means that if a public good is made available to one consumer, it is effectively made available to everyone. National defence is an example of a non-excludable good.

4   Non-excludability can give rise to a problem known as 'free-riding'. This is when some consumers fail to pay for the provision of the public good because they expect others will do so. This implies that the returns to potential suppliers will be less than society as a whole would be willing to pay collectively. So a market solution would imply too little public goods being produced to be socially optimal.

Externalities

5   'Externalities' result when a particular activity produces benefits or costs for other activities that are not directly priced into the market. Externalities are associated with, for example, research and development spill-overs, and environmental impacts, such as pollution. A firm might keep down its own costs by not investing in water pollution controls, but in so doing would raise the costs of those firms and individuals relying on using clean water. As a result the polluter has imposed an external cost on other users, or alternatively, a reduction in pollution confers an external benefit upon these other users.

Annex 1: Government Intervention

Imperfect Information

6	Information is needed for a market to operate efficiently. Buyers need to know the quality of the good or service to judge the value of the benefit it can provide. Sellers, lenders and investors need to know the reliability of a buyer, borrower or entrepreneur.

7	This information must be available fully to both sides of the market, and where it is not, market failure may result. This is known as 'asymmetry of information' and can arise in situations where, for example, sellers have information that buyers don't (or vice versa) about some aspect of product or service quality. Information asymmetry can restrict the quality of the good traded, resulting in 'adverse selection'. Another possible situation is where a contract or relationship places incentives upon one party to take (or not take) unobservable steps that are prejudicial to another party. This is known as 'moral hazard', an example of which is the tendency of people with insurance to reduce the care they take to avoid or reduce insured losses.

Market Power

8	Market power can arise as a result of insufficient actual or potential competition to ensure that the market continues to operate efficiently.

9	High start up costs can deter entry by competitors in the first place, and therefore create market power. This situation may be exacerbated through organisations acting strategically to protect their position in the market. Examples of this are when an organisation invests in any excess capacity available in the market, or engages in a practice known as 'predatory pricing' where prices are set low (e.g. below the marginal cost of production) to drive out competitors and then raised once they have left.

EQUITY

10	The other important rationale for government intervention is the achievement of equity objectives. Before acting, an assessment should be made of the extent of the inequality to be redressed, and the reasons it exists.

11	Further detail on the treatment of equality in project appraisal is provided in Annex 5.

ADDITIONALITY

12	The success of government intervention in terms of increasing output or employment in a given target area is usually assessed in terms of its 'additionality'. This is its net, rather than its gross, impact after making allowances for what would have happened in the absence of the intervention. Additionality can also be referred to as a 'supply side' or 'structural' impact, which operates by altering the productive capacity of the economy. This can occur either because of a change in the size of the workforce or a change in the productivity of the workforce. Examples of interventions that promote supply-side benefits include improving the working of markets and economic institutions, strengthening capabilities, and facilitating greater participation in the workforce. The extent to which a proposal may produce a supply side benefit is an important component of an appraisal.

13   If there are no grounds for expecting a proposal to have a supply side effect, any increase in government expenditure would result in a matching decrease in private expenditure, (known as 'crowding out'). If, however, the supply-side impact of a proposal is expected to be positive, the net additional impact on economic welfare will need to be measured. This may consist of additional employment or output, and constitutes a real net benefit which the appraisal should take into account.

14   Estimating this type of additionality will normally require an analysis of the product, labour, and in some cases, capital markets affected by the intervention. For example, when assessing the level of displacement of an employment creation programme or the impact of recruitment and redundancy decisions on a particular local area, it is necessary to examine the characteristics of the jobs created, or protected, in relation to the characteristics of the local labour market. They must then be compared with similar jobs in other local areas that are not subject to the policy. Such a comparison establishes the 'do nothing' case: what would have happened if the intervention had not gone ahead.

15   In some cases, the best source of information for assessing additionality may be from those who clearly have an interest in the outcome of the decision. In these circumstances, the information and forecasts should be confirmed by an independent source. For example, the implied growth in demand for services might be compared to other forecasts for the same region, and contrasted with past performance. Sensitivity analysis should also be carried out, using alternative values for the key variables.

16   After developing the 'do nothing' case, the next step is to assess the net impact or benefit of these different options. This net benefit is the 'additionality' of the option. Additionality must, however, be calculated with consideration of 'leakage', 'deadweight', 'displacement' and 'substitution' effects. These are explained below.

- 'Leakage' effects benefit those outside of the spatial area or group which the intervention is intended to benefit.

- 'Deadweight' refers to outcomes which would have occurred without intervention. Its scale can be estimated by assessing what would have happened in the 'do minimum' case, ensuring that due allowance is made for the other impacts which impact on net additionality.

- 'Displacement' and 'substitution' impacts are closely related. They measure the extent to which the benefits of a project are offset by reductions of output or employment elsewhere.

17   For example, a project may attract scarce skills, or investment, which would otherwise have gone to other parts of the country; or, if the policy involves support for local businesses, these may compete for resources and / or market share with non-assisted businesses.

18   The appropriate area for analysis of displacement effects will depend on the type of project. In the case of employment displacement, the area considered should usually approximate the local labour market.[1]

---

[1] Detailed guidance on methodologies for assessing displacement effects is available from the DTI Central Evaluation Team web site at http://www.dti.gov.uk. The recent DTI/ SBS evaluation of 'Smart', available on the same web site, provides an applied example. Also useful is research undertaken for DTI by the University of Durham (http://www.dur.ac.uk) and DWP's Travel to Work Areas.

Annex 1: Government Intervention

19 The effect on net employment and net output is likely to be much smaller than the direct employment and output effects of the project. Evidence should support the assessment of the scale and importance of any net employment and net output benefits, taking account of multiplier effects. A multiplier measures the further economic activity, (whether output or jobs), resulting from the creation of additional local economic activity. Where it is considered appropriate to calculate multipliers, guidance is available from English Partnerships and the Regional Development Agencies.[2]

> The net benefit of an intervention equals the gross benefits less the benefits that would have occurred in the absence of intervention (the 'deadweight') less the negative impacts elsewhere (including 'displacement' of activity), plus multiplier effects.

20 If there is no improvement in national economic efficiency, local employment and output effects, net of any local displacement effects, may be considered in parts of the appraisal where the project has a strong distributional rationale. For example, a policy may aim to reduce the rate of unemployment in a particular deprived area, as opposed to reducing the rate of unemployment overall.

21 Where potentially large changes to employment, (either as a result of employment creation, protection or redundancy) are concerned, assessment will normally require a thorough analysis of the local labour market. This should cover the age, skills and experience of those whose jobs are at stake, and how these compare with the characteristics of the unemployed and those who have recently found employment. The analysis might also assess the likelihood of new investment in the region in the event that these job losses occurred.

REGENERATION

22 Specific issues arise in the appraisal and evaluation of regeneration projects that have a rationale defined both in terms of their impact on efficiency and equity. In many cases, these projects are aimed at the regeneration of local areas, although some are targeted at entire regions.[3]

Regeneration Issues

23 When considering a regeneration proposal the following issues should be addressed:

- The rationale

    This needs to make clear:

    - Who the intended beneficiaries of the project are;
    - What are the mechanisms which will extend the benefits to them;

---

[2] For example, see 'Additionality: A Full Guide' (English Partnerships, 2001)

[3] More detail is provided in 'A Framework for the Evaluation of Regeneration Projects and Programmes', (EGRUP) available from HM Treasury, 1995 (currently under revision).

Annex 1: Government Intervention

- What structural benefits are expected as a result of the project; and,
- The means by which these will be achieved.

☐ The objectives

The objectives of regeneration programmes are likely to include improvements in one or more of the following:

- Labour supply and skills;
- Quality of life;
- Physical environment; and,
- Local business opportunities.

☐ Outcomes

These should be identified with respect to the relevant intermediate objectives. Regeneration outcomes might include:

- Reductions in crime;
- Improvements in the capacity of community organisations; or,
- Increases in local incomes and employment.

☐ Partnerships

Partnerships between the local community, business and government are important for the sustainability of regeneration projects and the well being of local communities. Most local regeneration projects involve partnerships, and are likely to have some effect on existing institutional relationships. An appraisal should include a description of the partnership and, where possible, its expected impact on the area.

Employment Impacts and Regeneration

24 Government intervention in the economy is sometimes undertaken with an employment objective in mind. In other cases, although employment is often retained as a principal objective, the justification for intervention is more far-reaching and the objectives tend to be more broadly cast. This is typical of regeneration projects.

25 Where programmes have multiple objectives, such as environmental improvements, these other additional benefits (and any associated costs) should be covered in the appraisal, together with employment impacts. The geographical focus of regeneration projects means that it is particularly important to assess displacement effects at both the local and national levels, particularly if the programme or project is substantial.

Annex 1: Government Intervention

State aids

26 State aids are transfers of state resources which provide selective support to particular companies. When the state confers even a limited advantage on an undertaking, there is usually a distortion, or risk of distortion, of competition. To protect competition across the EU, the European Commission provides a complex body of treaty-based legislation, frameworks and case law to establish which aid is, and is not allowable.

27 Aid is payable through a large variety of measures and instruments, including tax relief, soft loans and provisions to help prepare an undertaking for privatisation as well as grants and subsidies. As such, it is important that the state aid rules are considered from the onset of any proposal to ensure that proposed measures will be compatible with EU competition rules.

28 Further detail is available from the DTI and the European Commission.[4]

---

[4] See the DTI website (State Aid Policy Unit): http://www.dti.gov.uk and the European Commission's website on competition http://www.europa.eu.int.

VALUING NON-MARKET IMPACTS

ANNEX 2

INTRODUCTION

1   The valuation of non-market impacts is a challenging but important element of appraisal, and should be attempted wherever feasible. This Annex outlines techniques on how to value non-market impacts, and some typical applications such as time-savings, health benefits, prevented fatality, design quality, and the environment. These approaches can be complex but are equally as important as market impacts.

VALUING NON-MARKET IMPACTS

2   Where market values are not available for an identified cost or benefit, there are a number of approaches to attributing a value for inclusion in an appraisal, the most commonly used of which are outlined below.

Willingness to Pay and Willingness to Accept

3   The preferred method of valuation is to simulate the market by estimating the 'willingness to pay' (WTP) or 'willingness to accept' (WTA) a project's outputs or outcomes. Willingness to pay for a little more of a service is a reflection of the value placed by consumers on an increment of that service. The amount consumers are willing to pay depends to a large extent on the levels of income available to them, so valuations are usually obtained by averaging across income groups.

4   The quantification of potential social, health or environmental impacts normally requires an alternative approach to valuation. Techniques to establish money values for this type of non-market impact generally involve the inference of a price, through either a revealed preference or stated preference approach.

5   Revealed preference techniques involve inferring an implicit price revealed indirectly by examining consumers' behaviour in a similar or related market. Hedonic pricing is an example of this approach.[1] For example, the relationship between house prices and levels of environmental amenity, such as peace and quiet, may be analysed in order to assign a monetary value to the environmental benefit. Other examples are travel cost models (for recreational values) and random utility models (to value individual features of a site).

6   Stated preferences are normally obtained by specially constructed questionnaires and interviews designed to elicit estimates of the willingness to pay (WTP) for, or willingness to accept (WTA), a particular outcome.[2] When using stated preferences the main choice is between contingent valuation and choice modelling (CM). Contingent valuation studies elicit WTP or WTA via direct questions such as 'What is the maximum amount you would be prepared to pay every year to receive good x?' (the 'open-ended' format) or 'Which of the amounts listed below best describes your maximum willingness to pay every year to receive good x?' (the 'payment card' format). CM studies, on the other hand, elicit values by presenting respondents with a series of alternatives and then asking which is most preferred.[3]

---

[1] For more information on hedonic pricing see CSERGE publication, Day (2001) 'The Theory of Hedonic Markets; Obtaining Welfare Measures For Changes In Environmental Quality Using Hedonic Market Data': 'Report for the EU Working Group on Noise'.

[2] Guidance on the use of stated preference techniques can be obtained from 'Economic Valuation with Stated Preference Techniques: Summary Guide' available on the DfT website (http://:www.dft.gov.uk).

[3] The term Choice Modelling encompasses a range of stated preference techniques. The term includes choice experiments (often preferred because of their firm base in welfare economics), contingent ranking, contingent rating and paired comparisons. Further detail is contained in *Economic Valuation with Stated Preference Techniques: Summary Guide*, see DfT website: http://:www.dft.gov.uk.

Annex 2: Valuing Non-market Impacts

7 The technique chosen will depend on the individual circumstances, and should be judged on a case-by-case basis. As a general rule, revealed preference methods are fairly reliable, and should be used where the relevant information can be inferred. However, they cannot estimate the value placed on an asset by people who make no direct use of it. In these circumstances, stated preference methods may be helpful. In some cases, it will be appropriate to use both techniques together, for example, to check the consistency of results.

Other approaches

8 When faced with a mix of both monetary values and quantified data (and probably some unquantified considerations as well), weighting and scoring can be used to bring data expressed in different units into the appraisal process. Using this technique, options can be ranked and the preferred option identified. This approach usually involves an explicit relative weighting system for the different criteria relevant to the decision.[4] It often involves an implicit monetisation of different impacts, once the performance against the various criteria is compared to the costs considered worth spending to secure or to avoid them.

9 Where a direct assessment of the value of a benefit or cost is particularly uncertain, reference can be made to the costs of preventing the loss of, or replacing, a non-marketed good (such as a natural habitat or recreational facility). This does not provide a measure of its value but can provide a figure to focus discussion upon whether the good is worth as much as this expenditure.

10 In the absence of an existing reliable and accurate monetary valuation of an impact, a decision must be made whether to commission a study, and if so, how much resource to devote to the exercise. Key considerations that may govern a decision to commission research are:

- ❑ Tractability of the valuation problem: whether research is likely to yield a robust valuation;
- ❑ Range of application of the results of a study to future appraisals;
- ❑ How material the accuracy of the valuation is to the decision at hand. This may be gauged through sensitivity analysis around a range of plausible estimates; and,
- ❑ Scale of impact of the decision at hand. If the decision relates to a multi-billion pound programme or to regulation that will impose costs of similar scale upon industry, it is clearly worth devoting much more resource to ensuring that the valuations of the non-market benefits (and costs) are accurate than would be appropriate for a smaller scheme.

11 It is often difficult to assess the reliability of estimates emerging from a single study using a single method. Valuations may be unreliable because responses to questionnaires may be inconsistent or biased, or because valuations may take insufficient account of budget constraints. Estimates can be given more credence if different methods, or studies by different researchers, give similar results.

12 When using any technique, it is advisable to provide a range of values, and to subject the estimated values to a plausibility check with decision makers. The minimum or maximum valuation of a benefit or cost that would support a particular decision ('switching value') should be made explicit, compared with the real or implied valuations derived from previous decisions, and qualified by a statement of the robustness of the valuation techniques employed.

---

[4] An introduction to multi-criteria decision analysis – weighting and scoring – is given in *Multi-Criteria Analysis: A Manual* available from the ODPM website: http://www.odpm.gov.uk (see DTLR archive)

Annex 2: Valuing Non-market Impacts

CURRENT RESEARCH / PLAUSIBLE ESTIMATES

13 Following are some areas where research has been undertaken to derive plausible estimates for particular non-market costs and benefits.

Valuing Time

14 Within central government, the Department for Transport's (DfT) approach to valuing time in the appraisal of road schemes and other projects is well established.[5] This approach uses different values for 'employers' time and 'own' time (or working and non-working time).

15 The value of employees' time-savings (working) is the opportunity cost of the time to the employer. This will be equal at the margin to the cost of labour to the employer: the gross wage rate plus non-wage labour costs such as national insurance, pensions and other costs that vary with hours worked.[6]

16 The values for working time used in the appraisal and modelling of transport projects and policies, are based on the mileage weighted labour costs of users of each mode of transport. The National Travel Survey (NTS) contains detailed information on the distance and amount of time spent in travel by individuals in each earnings band to provide the appropriate weights for each mode of transport. The New Earnings Survey provides estimates of the earnings of drivers of commercial and public service vehicles. In theory, it is possible to collect data on the earnings of those who would use the project being appraised, although this is rarely practical.

17 It is accepted practice to use a national average standard value of non-working time (equity value of time-savings) for all modes of transport for appraisal purposes. The use of a project-specific value of non-working time might be preferable in cases where time-savings can be captured through revenue from fares. These will often form part of a commercial decision by, for example, a train operator assessing the case for accelerating a service.

18 For transport appraisals, journeys to and from work are included in non-working time. The value of savings in travel time for work is assumed to rise at roughly half the rate of real income.[7] For non-work time, this assumption balances a number of factors that might either tend to increase or decrease the value of time-savings relative to income. These might include a decline in the marginal utility of money as incomes increase, changes in the length of the working week and changes in the quality of travelling conditions.

19 Some additional considerations when valuing time-savings include:

- People place a higher value on saving walking or waiting time than on saving time spent in a vehicle. Evidence suggests that walking and waiting time should be valued at double that used for in-vehicle time.[8]

- Time spent in overcrowded conditions on public transport also carries a higher weight, the value being determined by the severity of the overcrowding.

---

[5] See DfT website for additional guidance: http://www.dft.gov.uk

[6] DTI uses 27 per cent as an adjustment for non-wage labour costs, while HSE uses 30 per cent. See Labour Cost Survey (LCS) 1992

[7] See DfT website: http://www.dft.gov.uk

[8] See DfT website: http://www.dft.gov.uk

Annex 2: Valuing Non-market Impacts

- Unreliability, measured in terms of deviations around the expected journey time, can also carry an additional penalty.

- Time-savings should be valued at the same rate per minute, whatever the extent of the saving or duration of the journey.

20 Using the estimated average values of travel time-savings from previous projects or proposals may not be appropriate if the characteristics of the client group are not similar to those of transport users, or if the circumstances differ significantly. Nevertheless, the estimates may serve as orders of magnitude.

Valuing Health Benefits

21 Health impacts are rarely a question simply of lives lost or saved. In policy areas that affect mainly health, an alternative approach is often used, to take account of changes in life expectancy (including expected life years where lives are lost or saved), and changes in the quality of life. This approach is known as the quality-adjusted life year (QALY).

22 The EuroQol instrument provides a simple and consistent framework for measuring general health and deriving QALY values and is the most commonly used measure of health benefits in Europe. It weights life expectancy for health-related quality of life over time.

23 The comparison of health interventions may reveal the impact of different factors on clinical effects. For example, working out the relationship between dosage and response of a particular medicine is a necessary prior step to properly valuing a policy for the provision of that medicine. In some cases, such as when the benefits of an intervention are measured in 'natural' units (e.g. reduced incidence of a disease or lower blood pressure rates), it may be appropriate to undertake an appraisal on the basis of its cost effectiveness.[9]

24 It is difficult to determine whether a health programme should be funded, or how large it should be, without first allocating a monetary value to the projected health gains. Valuation is also important when health impacts are to be weighed against non-health impacts. There are a number of techniques available, including undertaking a survey to estimate an individual's WTP for certain health benefits.[10] Once WTP is known, appraisers can compare the marginal benefits of an intervention against its marginal costs.

25 An example of a broad approach to estimating acute health impacts is set out in Box 2.1.[11]

---

[9] It is also possible to appraise a proposal on the basis of its 'cost utility' if there is an appropriate measure of the benefit of an intervention in terms of human welfare.

[10] The interim Interdepartmental Group on Costs and Benefits (IGCB) report, *'An Economic Analysis of the National Air Quality Strategy Objectives'* provides an example of how to conduct an economic analysis including health benefits.

[11] Further guidance on the assessment and valuation of health impacts is given in the Department of Health's (DH) *'Guidance on Policy Appraisal and Health'* (1995) and *'Evaluation of Health Technologies for Use in the NHS: Good Practice Guidelines'* (1999). HSE guidance on the valuation of health impacts is included in GAP23, *'Regulatory Impact Assessment – Policy Appraisal'*, June 2002.

Annex 2: Valuing Non-market Impacts

BOX 2.1: MEASURING SHORT TERM HEALTH BENEFITS ASSOCIATED WITH REDUCTIONS IN AIR POLLUTION[12]

A FIVE-STEP APPROACH TO VALUING HEALTH IMPACTS

1. Estimate the annual average concentration of pollutants and resident population in each 1km grid square of the country.

2. Assign the baseline level of the given health-related and pollution affected events to each grid square e.g., daily deaths, hospital admissions for the treatment of respiratory diseases.

3. Combine the data from (1) and (2) and apply a dose-response function linking pollutant concentrations with the relevant effects. Dose-response functions are expressed as a percentage increase in the baseline rate of health outcome per unit concentration of pollutant. Three outputs can be derived:

    3.1 The current effect on health of the relevant pollutant per grid square

    3.2 The benefit to health per grid square produced by the fall in concentrations of air pollutants expected to occur

    3.3 The benefit to health produced by reducing the concentration of pollutants in each grid square, in accordance with the proposed policies which aim to meet the objectives.

4. Sum the results obtained in (3) to estimate the total reduction in the number of cases of each health effect (which has an accepted dose-response function) associated with meeting or approaching the objectives.

5. Apply monetary values for each health effect to transform quantitative estimates into monetary estimates.

The Value of a Prevented Fatality or Prevented Injury

26 A benefit of some proposals is the prevention of fatalities or injuries. The appropriate starting point for valuing these benefits is to measure the individual's WTP for a reduction in risk of death (or their willingness to accept a new hazard and the ensuing increased risk).

27 The willingness of an individual to pay for small changes in their own or their household's risk of loss of life or injury can be used to infer the value of a prevented fatality (VPF). The changes in the probabilities of premature death or of serious injury used in such WTP studies are generally very small.[13]

---

[12] See *An Economic Analysis to Inform the Review of the Objectives for Particles Air Quality Strategy* available on the Defra website (http://www.defra.gov.uk).

[13] Franklin (2000), chapter 7, suggests that individuals systematically undervalue small risks, possibly introducing a downward bias in estimating VPF.

Annex 2: Valuing Non-market Impacts

28 In the UK, the main measure of VPF incorporates the 'extra' value placed on relatives and friends, and any further value placed by society on avoiding the premature death of individuals. Accordingly, the addition of an individual's WTP for the safety of others to his 'own' WTP for 'own' safety may lead to double counting.[14]

29 A lower bound on the value of a prevented fatality may be determined by revealed preference and stated preference studies. This lower bound is useful for determining a threshold of value for money for safety expenditure and also for comparing proposals concerning increased safety.

30 Revealed preference studies can derive individual WTP for risk reduction from, for example, the size of wage differentials for more or less risky occupations; or price versus safety trade-offs in choosing transport modes; or WTP for safety devices such as smoke alarms or car air bags. However, in practice, these estimates of the revealed value of a prevented fatality are not precise. Stated preference approaches have also been used to provide estimates of VPF using questionnaires.[15]

31 In the UK, the Department for Transport (DfT) values the reduction of the risk of death in the context of road transport at about £1.145m per fatal casualty prevented (in 2000 prices).[16] In addition to the WTP measures, these estimates include gross lost output, medical and ambulance costs. Values are uprated in line with assumed changes in GDP per head.

32 DfT also attributes monetary values to the prevention of non-fatal casualties, based on a WTP approach. Serious and slight casualties are valued separately and the values are uprated in line with changes in GDP per head. Values currently in use for preventing a serious and slight road injury are £128,650 and £9,920 respectively (at 2000 prices).[17] Costs of police, insurance and property damage are added to these casualty values to obtain values for the prevention of road accidents. The HSE tariff of monetary values for pain, grief and suffering begins at £150 for the most minor non-reportable injury.[18]

33 There is evidence that individuals are not indifferent to the cause and circumstances of injury or fatality. For example, in their estimate of benefits from asbestos proposals, HSE currently doubles the VPF figure to allow for individual aversion to dying from cancer, and the additional associated personal and medical costs.[19]

Valuing Design Quality

34 Design quality is an important element of all public sector building projects and should be assessed during appraisal. Limiting property valuation to traditional methods without consideration of the costs and benefits of design investment can distort the decision making process. Good design will not always result in the lowest initial capital cost. However, over the period of the contract a higher initial investment can, when expressed as a discount value, result in the lower whole life costs.

---

[14] This augmentation of the 'own' WTP-based figure is legitimate only if concern for others' safety takes the form of 'safety-focused altruism' where despite being concerned for others' safety, people are indifferent to other determinants of their overall well-being. For cases that are intermediate, some augmentation of the 'own' WTP-based figure is justifiable. (M W Jones-Lee, (1992))

[15] For additional information, refer to HSE (2000a), 'Valuation of Benefits of Health and Safety Control, Final Report', which describes an approach used to update the DfT value for reduction in risk of a fatality.

[16] DfT See (Highways Economic Note No 1. 2000) 'Valuation of The Benefits of Prevention of Road Accidents And Casualties'. Available on the DfT website (http://www.dft.gov.uk).

[17] ibid

[18] See HSE website: http://www.hse.gov.uk

[19] There is currently no evidence to support this adjustment. HSE has commissioned a study to investigate public preferences for preventing fatalities due to 'dreaded' risks to inform this issue.

Annex 2: Valuing Non-market Impacts

35   The benefits of good design include:

- Simplification and savings in cost, by ensuring that capital costs are competitive and that savings can be achieved on running costs;
- Increased output and quality of service through enhancement of the environment in which a service is provided; and
- Staff recruitment and retention.

36   Where good design has a direct economic impact, such as staff retention or patient recovery times, it may be possible to calculate the costs and benefits directly. However, it is often difficult, if not impossible, to calculate the monetary value of many of the benefits of good design, such as civic pride, educational achievement or user experience. In such instances, it may be necessary to use contingent valuation or a similar technique. For smaller projects, where contingent valuation may prove too complicated, research studies can help with comparisons and benchmarking to ensure good design is accounted for.

> **DETAILED GUIDANCE ON EVALUATING AND DELIVERING DESIGN QUALITY CAN BE FOUND IN:**
> - *The Value of Good Design*, CABE
> - *Achieving Well Designed Schools Through PFI*, CABE
> - *Better Civic Buildings and Space*, CABE
> - *Treasury Guidance Note 7: How to Achieve Design Quality in PFI projects*
> - *Improving Standards of Design in the Procurement of Public Buildings*, CABE/OGC
> - *The CABE website* (http://www.cabe.org.uk)

VALUING ENVIRONMENTAL IMPACTS

37   The valuation of environmental costs and benefits is constantly evolving, with new research continually being funded by the UK government and its agencies. Research covers both methodological development and the estimation of values. There are a number of valuable reference sources that discuss valuation issues in depth.[20] The following paragraphs provide information on government research and guidance on the quantification and monetisation of impacts, including which departments are sponsoring research. As this is a developing field, policy makers are encouraged to refer to the Green Book homepage, in order to locate the most up to date information.

---

[20] See, for example, "Economic Valuation with Stated Preference Techniques: Summary Guide", available on the DfT website at http://www.dft.gov.uk.

Annex 2: Valuing Non-market Impacts

Impacts of policies and measures on greenhouse gas emissions

38 Current methodologies for assessment of the effects of policies and measures on greenhouse gas emissions are policy specific with no standard guidance available. There are some models available that can be used to assess the effects of particular types of proposals on emissions (e.g. National Road Traffic Forecasts).[21]

39 The impact of a new policy, project or programme on emissions should be expressed in terms of carbon savings, or in terms of additional emissions, measured in million tonnes of carbon-dioxide equivalent (MtC02).

40 In cases where quantification of the climate change effect is impractical, an assessment of whether the policy is likely to increase or decrease emissions, combined with a qualitative assessment of the significance of this change, should be included in the appraisal.

41 Once the emissions impact of a proposal has been quantified, current research informs the calculation of illustrative values for the social damage cost of carbon.[22] This can then be used to estimate the monetary value of the impacts.

Assessing vulnerability to the impacts of climate change

42 In 1997, the UK government established the UK Climate Impacts Programme (UKCIP) to help public and private organisations assess their vulnerability to climate change. UKCIP, together with Defra, can provide the latest information on climate change predictions and assessments. This includes guidance on how to identify and assess the risks and uncertainties posed by a changing climate, and a methodology for costing the impacts of climate change.

43 Key policy areas where climate change might be a particularly important consideration include: investment appraisal for long-term planning and infrastructure projects, regulatory and planning frameworks, contingency planning and long-term policy frameworks.

Air Quality

44 Assessing the impact of particular policies on air quality is a complex science. Sophisticated modelling tools exist to forecast emissions from different sources and estimate the impact on ambient concentration levels of different pollutants at different locations.[23] Government departments and agencies may need to consider air quality impacts in the design of their policies. For example, the Highways Agency's Design Manual for Roads and Bridges can be used to forecast the impact of new or existing road schemes on emissions of key pollutants from road transport.

45 Impacts on air quality are generally expressed in terms of either the total volume change in emissions of a particular pollutant from a particular source; the likely impact of this change on levels of ambient air quality in the affected area; or the total number of households likely to be affected by these changes.

---

[21] Contact Defra for further advice on assessing the effects of a proposal on emissions.

[22] A Government Economic Service working paper 'Estimating the Social Cost of Carbon Emissions' suggests illustrative values for the social damage cost of carbon that can be used to estimate the monetary value of impacts once they have been quantified. A copy of this working paper is available on the Treasury's website http://www.hm-treasury.gov.uk. Defra can provide an associated guidance note on how to use these values in policy appraisal.

[23] For a technical reference on the approach to air quality mapping and modelling, see "The Air Quality Strategy for England, Scotland, Wales and Northern Ireland", Defra, January 2000,

Annex 2: Valuing Non-market Impacts

46   In cases where detailed modelling is not possible, a reasoned statement of whether or not a particular policy is likely to result in greater or lesser emissions of particular pollutants should be included in the appraisal.

47   Research has been funded to develop a methodology for quantifying and monetising, where appropriate, the health and environmental impacts of air quality changes.[24]

Landscape

48   Landscape includes townscape, heritage, and other related matters. Guidelines for assessing the impact of policies, projects and programmes on landscape have been devised by English Heritage and the Countryside Commission.[25] The Commission for Architecture and the Built Environment (CABE) may also be able to provide guidance.[26]

49   Research has also been commissioned Defra to estimate the value of environmental landscape features associated with agri-environment schemes. Contingent valuation techniques have been used, producing an Environmental Landscape Features (ELF) model. This constitutes a first attempt at a benefits transfer tool for appraising agri-environment policy.[27] Features covered include heather moorland, rough grazing, field margins and hedgerows. The model provides estimates of WTP for these features on an area basis, and estimates of their diminishing marginal utility.

Water

50   It is not easy to derive economic values for damage costs of water pollutants. The complexity of the way in which pollutants entering the water environment affect chemical water quality and ecological status means that it is difficult to devise simple dose-response functions. Furthermore, there are several ways in which the benefits of improving water quality are location-dependent and it is not easy to determine the relevant population to use for grossing up values, or how to take account of decay functions to represent 'distance decay'.[28] Therefore, water valuation studies do not generally produce 'marginal damage cost' estimates for specific pollutants; they are more geared towards producing values for observable changes in environmental quality.

51   Numerous studies have attempted to estimate the economic value of changes to water quality or flow rates/levels in water bodies,[29] but establishing values that can be transferred is difficult. New research is planned by Defra, the Environment Agency and Ofwat to value the environmental benefits of changes in water quality.

---

[24] Guidance can be found on the Defra website (http://www.defra.gov.uk). Defra has also sponsored research to generate empirical estimates of UK WTP for reductions in health risks associated with air pollution.

[25] These guidelines draw extensively on the Guidance on the Methodology for Multi-Modal Studies (GOMMMS) available from the DTLR archive accessed from the ODPM website: http://www.odpm.gov.uk.

[26] See website: http://www.cabe.org.uk

[27] "Estimating the Value of Environmental Features", Reports to MAFF, January 1999 and June 2001.

[28] "Distance decay" refers to the observation that people living further away from an environmental impact care less about it and therefore express lower valuations.

[29] For example, "Valuation of Benefits to England and Wales of a Revised Bathing Water Quality Directive and Other Beach Characteristics Using the Choice Experiment Methodology", Eftec report to Defra, 2002. Also, the Environment Agency has a register of 50 water valuation studies which covers values for recreation, water quality, flood defence, navigation and fishing (Netcen 1998).

Biodiversity

52 The benefits of biodiversity can be difficult to measure, define and value. However, if these benefits are disregarded or given a low priority in appraisal work, there is a risk of excessive and potentially irreversible degradation of natural resource stocks.

53 Defra and the Forestry Commission fund research on the valuation of biodiversity that is concerned both with developing methodological approaches and deriving empirical estimates.[30]

Noise

54 Assessing the impact of noise can be complex, not least because of the subjective nature of many of its effects. Despite this, a number of approaches to quantifying the impact of changes in noise according to the source, the scale and nature of the proposals have been developed. For example, the impact of new transport infrastructure or industrial developments can be quantified according to the number of people/households affected by an increase or decrease of noise levels measured in average decibels (dB(A)). This approach can also be used to assess the impact of changes to traffic control measures.

55 This is a rapidly developing area and studies are being taken forward to obtain monetary values for noise.[31] Recent studies across Europe have yielded a range of values, many of which lie in the range of €20 - 30 per household per decibel per year. The median value from those studies is €23.5 per household per decibel per year (2001 prices).[32]

Recreational and amenity values for forests

56 In 1992, the Forestry Commission established a value for recreational visitors to forests of £1 per visit. More recent work on the recreational value of forests in Northern Ireland suggested that mean willingness-to-pay (WTP) varies between £0.60 and £1.74 per visit, depending upon the location of the forest, its attributes and socio-economic characteristics of the visitors.[33] If a high level of accuracy is required, recreational values need to be more sensitive to the attributes of individual forests, the location and availability of substitutes, and the characteristics of the visitors in the catchment area. However if a broader estimate is sufficient, the 1992 value (£1 per visit) indexed to the year of the appraisal should suffice.

57 The Forestry Commission commissioned a further study to estimate the range of non-market benefits associated with forestry. This reviewed existing methodologies and research to determine the best approach to valuing the non-market benefits of UK forestry and made recommendations on non-market values for recreation, landscape, amenity, biodiversity and carbon sequestration.[34]

---

[30] Guidance is also available from two OECD publications, "Handbook of biodiversity valuation: a guide for policy makers" and "Valuation of Biodiversity Benefits: Selected Studies."

[31] The results of DfT noise studies in the UK and guidance on how to implement values when undertaking appraisal are published on the DfT and Defra websites.

[32] Summarised in the 2002 report to the European Commission DG Environment "The State of the Art on Economic Valuation of noise" by Stale Navrud .

[33] Summarised in a report to the Forestry Commission. "Non-Market Benefits of Forestry, Phase 1". (See http://www.forestry.gov.uk)

[34] ibid.

Valuing disamenity

58 Activities including the transport and disposal of waste and the quarrying of minerals and aggregates give rise to a range of undesirable impacts that can undermine public enjoyment of an area. A number of studies have attempted to value these, which together can be considered disamenity impacts and which may include noise, traffic disturbance, dust, odours and visual intrusion.

59 The former DETR commissioned a study to inform the decision on whether to impose a tax on aggregates and, if so, at what level (See Box 2.2). [35]

BOX 2.2: SUMMARY OF DETR STUDY

The study estimated how much people valued avoiding the adverse environmental effects of quarrying for construction aggregates, such as crushed rock, sand and gravel, both in their locality and in landscapes of national importance.

Ten thousand respondents were picked at random from areas surrounding 21 sample quarries and other extraction sites. They were asked how much they would be willing to pay, in the form of increased taxes over a five year period, for the local quarry to be shut down, assuming that the site was restored in keeping with the surrounding landscape, and that the workers found new employment. A further 1,000 respondents, chosen at random from 21 English postcodes not near aggregates production sites, were asked what they would be willing to pay to close a quarry in a National Park (the Peak District and the Yorkshire Dales were used as examples). These results show the value attributed to the environmental damages of quarrying by people not themselves directly affected.

The environmental effects which people were asked to value included: adverse effects on nature, such as loss of biodiversity; noise from quarry transport and blasting; traffic and dust levels; and visual intrusion.

From the results of the surveys, national estimates were calculated for the average amount that people are willing to pay for the environmental benefits obtained from early closure of a quarry. These are shown below for each category of sample site:

'Willingness to Pay' estimates:

Case Study Sites	£/tonne
Hard rock	0.34
Sand and Gravel	1.96
Quarries in National Parks	10.52

The national average amount which individuals were willing to pay for the closure of all types of quarry sites, weighted by the type of output, was calculated to be £1.80 per tonne.

---

[35] London Economics (1999) *The External Costs and Benefits of the Supply of Aggregates: Phase II*. Report for DETR, now found on the ODPM website (see http://www.odpm.gov.uk)

Annex 2: Valuing Non-market Impacts

LAND AND BUILDINGS

ANNEX 3

INTRODUCTION

1   This annex contains sections on the valuation of land and buildings. It discusses how the value of property rights should be taken into account and provides a worked example (see Box 3.1) to show how the techniques discussed apply.

ACQUISITION AND USE OF PROPERTY

Valuing Property Rights

2   Appraising for projects involving interests in land and buildings is complicated by the longevity of the freehold and leasehold interests and the durability of the assets. This section discusses these issues.

3   Many appraisals involve considering the optimisation of government interests in land and buildings. The appraisals will involve interests in leasehold and freehold properties, PFI/ PPP arrangements where property forms a part, and direct investment in construction.[1]

4   Securing value for money from existing investments, as well as new public infrastructure requires careful consideration. With existing assets, consideration needs to be given as to whether these can be surrendered, merged or modified to release value. With newly built assets, consideration has to be given to design, whole life costs, fitness for purpose, operational efficiency, and end of life costs as well as the initial impact of the capital payment.

5   If a proposal involves the acquisition, management or disposal of legal rights in land and buildings, the value of those property rights needs to be taken into account, whether these interests are freehold, leasehold, a licence, or subsumed within a PPP/ PFI contract. With new construction, the initial cost, lifetime costs and residual value will need to be considered.

6   Property interests are costed in terms of capital value, or rental value. Some leasehold interests, where the rental is different from the market value, may also have a capital value. Appraisals normally use capital values when appraising freehold property, properties with development value, and longer leasehold interests. As for other appraisals, this is done by bringing the cashflows to a net present value or net present cost.

The Basis Of Valuation

7   The valuation of a site should be based on the most valuable possible use, rather than the highest value that could be obtained for its current use. The valuation should include an assessment of the social costs and benefits of alternative uses of a site, not just the market value.

Obtaining Valuations

8   An assessment of the value of a site in the most valuable alternative use should be based on the advice of suitably qualified and experienced valuation surveyor.[2] Either in-house valuers or external experts can be commissioned to carry out the valuation.

---

[1] New orders obtained by contractors from the public sector totaled £6,176 million in 2000 (Construction Statistics Annual 2000 DTI, Table 1.1, pg. 16 and Table 1.4, page 20).

[2] For instance, a corporate member of the Royal Institution of Chartered Surveyors or the Institute of Revenues, Rating and Values.

Annex 3: Land and Buildings

9 Valuations should be based on the definitions of 'market value' (MV) or 'open market value' (OMV) used in the '*RICS Appraisal and Valuation Manual*'. Valuations should take into consideration the prospects for development and the presence of any purchaser with a special interest, insofar as the market would do so. To take into account such potential purchasers, it may be necessary in instructing the valuer to adapt the RICS definition of MV/ OMV.

Common Issues In Valuation

10 The value of an interest in property depends on the use for which it is being valued (e.g. as residences, shops or offices), the physical state of the asset, the duration of the legal interest, and obligations such as rents and repairs, etc.

11 Normally, as noted above, the alternative use with the highest market value should be considered. To assess the highest value reasonably obtainable, the valuer must consider the market demand for that use together with the planning situation.

12 Where the development property has planning consent for a more valuable use, the valuation should reflect the market demand for that use. If the appraiser believes that there is the prospect of planning consent for an even more valuable use than that previously obtained, and that there is a real economic demand for that use, then the appraisal should ignore both the existing use of the building and the existing planning consent. Instead, it should normally reflect the best use and highest value of the site, in the way that the market would do.

13 If there is no planning approval, the potential for obtaining such approval should be estimated, and reflected in the valuation. Alternatively, the value of a property may be depressed by restrictions on development. It should be considered whether or not these can be lifted (and at what cost), and the result of this should be reflected in the valuation. In all cases, the prospect for obtaining a higher planning consent should be considered by the appraiser and his professional property advisor.

14 Valuations based on market prices reflect private, rather than social, costs and benefits. Accordingly, they will not always take into full account the actual or potential amenity value, or environmental impact, of a particular land use. Generally, where there is such an impact (for example along the route of a proposed new road), land should be valued at its market price. Environmental costs or benefits of a change of use that are not captured in the market price should also be included in the reckoning.

15 Where the current use of land is subsidised, it is sometimes necessary to adjust market prices to reflect the impact of the subsidy. In particular, when considering transferring land from agricultural use, it will generally be appropriate to make a downward adjustment to the market price of the land to reflect the capitalised impact of expected future UK and EU subsidies: i.e. the land should be priced net of the impact of such subsidies.

16 As these adjustments reflect avoided future costs to taxpayers, it is the adjusted sum that should be included in the assessment.

17 Assessing the value of buildings in their most profitable use is fairly straightforward where the building can be readily adapted to different user requirements, such as standard office accommodation. However, many public sector buildings (such as prisons and hospitals) may not be so easily adaptable to other purposes.

18 Even if there is no developed market for a particular type of property, there may be relevant market information. Such evidence might come from market transactions from the sale, or lettings of buildings or part of buildings such as in the private hospital sector, letting of accommodation for tribunals, etc. It is desirable to estimate

Annex 3: Land and Buildings

value as close to objective market transactions evidence as possible. However, there are some public sector buildings (such as prisons and defence installations) that may not be easily adaptable to other purposes.

19 If there is no alternative use for the buildings, the property should be valued as the higher of:

- The value of the site, cleared of buildings and contamination and ready for redevelopment; or
- The value of the site and buildings in its current use.

Valuations Where There Is No Market

20 The valuation of a specialised building for which there is no market is problematic for valuers and appraisers. The RICS *Appraisal and Valuation Manual* suggests using the 'Depreciated Replacement Cost' basis of valuation.

21 Depreciated Replacement Cost (DRC) comprises the 'open market value' of the land in the present use, plus the current gross replacement cost of the buildings and their site works. The buildings costs are depreciated by an allowance to reflect their condition and age, and their functional, economic and environmental obsolescence. These factors render the existing property less valuable than a new replacement.

22 Valuers have two approaches to depreciated replacement cost. One involves envisaging an exact replacement of the existing building, which can be artificial if the skills and materials do not actually exist to replicate that building. The second approach is to imagine a modern building that is a functional substitute, even if it is smaller, or differently configured to reflect modern circumstances.

23 DRC valuations are relatively specialised and advice should be sought from a professional property consultant. DRC figures are subjective figures, which reflect the value to the owner, rather than objective, transaction based, opportunity cost. They tend to be on the high side and require careful handling. DRC should only be used where there is a continuing operational need for the property (or the stream of services derived from it) over the period of the appraisal.

LEASES AND RENTS

24 Sometimes, the actual rent paid on leasehold property (the 'passing rent') will vary from the market rent. This most often occurs in older long leases with unusual rent review patterns. In longer leases with infrequent rent reviews, the market rent can substantially exceed the passing rent and this difference is known as a 'profit rent'. This lasts until the next rent review or the lease ends. This can give the lease a capital value in its own right and such leases are sold from time to time. In a depressed market, the passing rent can exceed the market rent so that the property is described as 'over-rented'. Such leases usually contain upward only rent review clauses (UORR) so that if a rent is set at the top of a property cycle, this may persist over one or more rent review periods.

25 The market rent is the estimated amount for which a property would lease at the date of the appraisal between a willing lessor and a willing lessee operating at arms length, after proper marketing, with proper market knowledge, prudently and without compulsion.

26 Appraisers should also note that the passing rental value (and thus the capitalised rental value) on physically similar properties might be quite different. This may reflect the fact that the lease of one office block may be on full

Annex 3: Land and Buildings

repairing and ensuring terms where the tenant pays for all repairs and insurance. A physically identical office block may have an entirely different lease but with the landlord responsible for insurance and repairs.

27   It is important to remember that what is being valued is the legal interest in a property rather than the physical property itself. This means that appraisers should generally use the market rent because the legal interest that is being appraised will usually cover a number of rent review periods, and it will be the market rent that, over time, will be the relevant value. However, where UORR clauses are imposed, it would be incorrect to use sensitivity testing to show the impact of falling market rents, as the actual rent paid will not fall in line with the market.

DISPOSAL OF PROPERTY

28   Departments have a duty to dispose of property surplus to requirements within three years and should not hold land speculatively. They are encouraged to obtain professional, specialist advice when doing this. The sale of freehold property, or the assignment or subletting of leasehold property, is likely to involve significant costs, (e.g. legal fees, marketing costs and removal costs). Situations can be complex where there is more than one occupier.

29   One question to consider is what should be done to a surplus property prior to putting it on the market. Initiatives to improve its marketability would include:

- Refurbishment;
- Applying for a different outline (or detailed) planning consent. However, sometimes it is not clear what is the best alternative use, in which case properties could be put on the market 'subject to planning permission'; and
- Consulting other public sector bodies about their property requirements. The OGC maintains a register of property surpluses and requirements.

30   More detailed advice on property disposals can be obtained from the Office of Government Commerce (OGC).[3]

COST-EFFECTIVE LAND USE

31   The plots of land that are available for new developments may not precisely match requirements, but where a plot exceeds requirements, the surplus should be disposed of as soon as possible.

32   An exception to this rule is in cases where future expansion is anticipated, (for example within a phased development), and where the extra land may not be available later. Efforts should still be made to secure some return from land than needs to be retained, but which is temporarily surplus (for example by short term letting).

33   Including the value of land already owned means that an appraisal must also include the costs of retaining vacant land. It is sometimes argued that vacant land on government sites could not be used for any other purpose because of the demands of security, and so the opportunity cost of this land is zero. However, it is generally possible, by the re-organisation of a land portfolio taken as a whole, to release land elsewhere. In practice, land that can be used for a public sector project nearly always has an opportunity cost.

---

[3] http://www.ogc.gov.uk and from '*Government Accounting*', particularly Chapter 24, Disposal of Assets

Annex 3: Land and Buildings

BOX 3.1: LAND AND BUILDINGS WORKED EXAMPLE

34 The purpose of this example is to introduce basic concepts regarding typical accommodation appraisals and/or evaluations; some are specific to land and property valuation, and others apply more generally.

CONTEXT

A government department (A) owns the freehold of a 2000 m2, 1960's office block on the outskirts of the city. It lets 500 m2 to another government department (B) under a memorandum of terms. Department B continues to occupy the premises, with Department A's permission, although the current memorandum of terms has expired. Department A occupies the remainder.

Enquiries of the local authority have confirmed that planning consent for conversions of the buildings for high density, high quality residential development would be granted. Department A's current accommodation is poor; a staff survey has revealed widespread dissatisfaction with its facilities. Managers are now exploring the options for providing future accommodation needs.

OBJECTIVES

The main aim of Department A is to provide modern office accommodation for its staff in a manner which represents value for money.

OPTIONS

A number of options are being considered, including relocating the activities of this branch to the Department A's head office. For this example, only three will be considered in detail.

Option 1 'Do Minimum'

This entails refurbishing the current property at a cost of £1 million. Department B has expressed an interest in taking a new lease after refurbishment for 15 years, with 5 yearly upwards-only rent reviews at a rent of £60,000 per annum, effectively on full repairing and insuring terms, which represents the current open market rental value.

It is likely that there will be a need for a further minor refurbishment of the building in 10 year's time at a cost of £0.5 million, but it is anticipated that this will help maintain the open market rental value of the property in real terms, with only a slight decline.

Option 2 New office block

Department A moves into 1500m2 of a new city centre office block, to be completed in the near future, situated next door to a rail and bus terminus. The location is seen as one that will improve markedly over the next couple of years or so and consequently, rental values are expected to grow faster than the rate of inflation over this period.

continued

Annex 3: Land and Buildings

BOX 3.1: LAND AND BUILDINGS WORKED EXAMPLE (contd)

The developer would be prepared to accept a fifteen-year full repairing and insuring lease for the property, with a tenant's option to break at the end of the 10th year, without penalty. The initial rent can be agreed today at £240,000 per annum subject to upwards-only rent reviews every 5 years. Department A's consultant surveyors have confirmed that the rent and other terms generally reflect current market conditions.

Option 3 Re-use existing vacant government office space

Department A moves to a vacant office property currently leased to another department and surplus to their requirements.

The property, known as Crown Building, comprises a 1500m2 modern city center office block. The location is similar to that of the new city centre property outlined in Option 2 above. The passing rent is lower at £200,000 as it is a second hand building with a more basic specification, but growth assumptions are similar.

The existing 15 years' lease has 5 years left to run and can be renewed under the Security of Tenure provisions of the Landlord and Tenant Act. The Owning Department's agents advise that the cost of disposal or surrender will be equivalent to the rent and running costs for the remaining period of the lease.

ASSUMPTIONS

The detailed assumptions are shown in the notes to the tables of calculations.

Option appraisal

The Department initially performs a cost-effectiveness analysis on the three options. Table 1 shows the results of this analysis.

Initial appraisal findings (table 1)

The cost effectiveness analysis shows that option 3, the reuse option, provided significantly better value.

Valuing benefits (table 2)

Managers want to investigate the differences between the options further. Models are developed of the benefits that accrue from each option. There are some additional benefits in moving to the new, more accessible site. These include times-savings for the public who use the site regularly, accruing from the more central location.

CONCLUSION

In this example, cost effectiveness analysis is sufficient to make an appropriate choice. Valuing its additional benefits further improves the case for developing a solution based on Option 3.

This example illustrates some specific aspects of accommodation appraisals, as well as introducing benefits valuation in the appraisal process, which is considered in more detail in Annex 2.

Annex 3: Land and Buildings

Land and Buildings Worked Example: Table 1
COST EFFECTIVENESS ANALYSIS

Reference to Notes		TOTAL	Year 0	1	2	3	4	5	6	7	8	9	10	11	12	13	14	15
	Option 1 Do minimum - refurbish																	
	Property/capital costs																	
1	Rent received (nominal terms)		0.0	30.0	60.0	60.0	60.0	60.0	67.1	67.1	67.1	67.1	67.1	75.9	75.9	75.9	75.9	75.9
2 & 3	Rent received (real terms - year 0 prices)		0.0	29.6	57.8	56.4	55.0	53.7	58.5	57.1	55.7	54.4	53.0	58.5	57.1	55.7	54.4	53.0
4	Site value		-3,500															3,200
5	Refurbishment costs		-1,000										-500					
6	*Running costs*																	
	Rates (real terms)			-103	-105	-108	-110	-113	-116	-119	-122	-125	-128	-131	-134	-138	-141	-145
	Maintenance/repairs			-30	-30	-30	-30	-30	-30	-30	-30	-30	-30	-30	-30	-30	-30	-30
7	Utilities/other			75	-100	-100	-100	-100	-100	-100	-100	-100	-100	-100	-100	-100	-100	-100
8	Costs of holding Crown Building vacant			-295	-290	-286	-281	-277										
9	Tenants' service charge contribution			12	12	12	12	12	12	12	12	12	12	12	12	12	12	12
	Business costs																	
	Business travel and courier costs			-130	-130	-130	-130	-130	-130	-130	-130	-130	-130	-130	-130	-130	-130	-130
	CASHFLOW	-4,500	-441	-585	-585	-584	-584	-305	-310	-314	-319	-823	-238	-325	-330	-335	2,860
10	Net present cost @ 3.5%	-7,692	-4,500	-433	-556	-537	-518	-501	-253	-248	-243	-238	-594	-166	-219	-215	-211	1,737
	Option 2 New City Centre Block																	
	Property/capital costs																	
11	Rent paid (nominal terms)			-180	-240	-240	-240	-240	-313	-313	-313	-313	-313	-354	-354	-354	-354	-354
11 & 12	Rent paid (real terms - year 0 prices)			-178	-231	-226	-220	-215	-273	-266	-260	-254	-247	-273	-266	-260	-254	-247
	Fitting out, telecoms, removals		-250															
13	Tenants' compensation		-120															
	Dilapidations on lease expiry																	-250
	Running costs																	
	Rates			-128	-131	-135	-138	-141	-145	-149	-152	-156	-160	-164	-168	-172	-177	-181
	Maintenance/repairs			-20	-20	-20	-20	-20	-20	-20	-20	-20	-20	-20	-20	-20	-20	-20
	Utilities/other (cleaning/security)			-85	-85	-85	-85	-85	-85	-85	-85	-85	-85	-85	-85	-85	-85	-85
	Costs of holding Crown Building vacant			-295	-290	-286	-281	-277										
	Business costs																	
	Business travel and courier costs			-90	-90	-90	-90	-90	-90	-90	-90	-90	-90	-90	-90	-90	-90	-90
	CASHFLOW	-370	-796	-848	-841	-834	-828	-613	-610	-607	-605	-602	-632	-629	-627	-625	-873
	Net present cost @ 3.5%	-8,732	-370	-782	-805	-772	-739	-709	-507	-488	-469	-451	-434	-440	-424	-408	-393	-530
	Option 3 Reuse Crown Building																	
	Property/capital costs																	
11	Rent paid (nominal terms)		-200	-200	-200	-200	-200	-261	-261	261	-261	-261	-295	295	295	295	295
11 & 12	Rent paid (real terms - year 0 prices)			-198	-193	-188	-183	-179	-228	-222	-217	-211	-206	-228	222	217	211	206
	Fitting out, telecoms, removals		-750															
13	Tenants' compensation		-120															
	Dilapidations on lease expiry																	-250
	Running costs																	
	Rates			-103	-105	-108	-110	-113	-116	-119	-122	-125	-128	-131	-134	-138	-141	-145
	Maintenance/repairs			-25	-25	-25	-25	-25	-25	-25	-25	-25	-25	-25	-25	-25	-25	-25
	Utilities/other (cleaning/security)			-85	-85	-85	-85	-85	-85	-85	-85	-85	-85	-85	-85	-85	-85	-85
	Business costs																	
	Business travel and courier costs			-90	-90	-90	-90	-90	-90	-90	-90	-90	-90	-90	-90	-90	-90	-90
	CASHFLOW	-870	-500	-498	-496	-494	-492	-543	-541	-538	-536	-534	-559	-113	-121	-130	-389
	Net present cost @ 3.5%	-6,094	-870	-492	-473	-455	-438	-422	-450	-432	-416	-400	-385	-389	-76	-79	-82	236
		0	1	2	3	4	5	6	7	8	9	10	11	12	13	14	15

THE GREEN BOOK 75

Annex 3: Land and Buildings

NOTES TO TABLE 1 – EXPLANATIONS AND ASSUMPTIONS

1. 'Passing rent' (nominal) and real rental values ('market rent'). In this example, rent is reviewed every 5 years. This means that the real rent level is eroded by inflation between rent reviews; inflation is assumed to be 2.5%, as is the market rental growth rate (i.e. rents rise in line with inflation). For example, in year 6, actual rent (the passing rent) catches up with the market rent (the calculation is 60,000*1.025^4.5=67,052).

   There are two main methods to deal with rental cash flows – (a) convert the nominal cash flow into the real terms by deflating the rent by the rate of inflation and then discount at the appropriate discount rate, or (b) discount the nominal cash flow at the 'double discount' rate, which is derived by multiplying the discount rate with the inflation rate. The Treasury's preferred method (as shown in this example) is (a), which is more explicit, allowing all the cash flows to be gathered together and expressed under a common term. However, the results produced are identical.

2. Rental growth is assumed to be 2.5% for Option 1: no higher than inflation.

3. Rent-free period: The tenant will enjoy a rent-free period of 6 months in year 1 (as part of the terms negotiated for the new lease).

4. Site value. This is the opportunity cost of not selling the site at its open market value in the best alternative use (i.e. for residential accommodation).

5. Running costs inflate annually and therefore can be expressed in real terms relating to year 1.

6. Utilities costs reduce in real terms from Option 1 to 2 because of energy and environmental efficiencies of the new building.

7. Other costs also reduce in real terms from Option 1 to 2 because of other efficiencies (location and scale).

8. Tenants contribution: tenants will contribute towards some of the cost of the ten-year refurbishment.

9. Business travel costs reduce from Option 1 to 2 because of the more accessible location of the new building.

10. Cash flows and net present costs. The net present costs are shown using the 3.5% discount rate.

11. Rental growth = 10% during the first two years, 2.5% thereafter; this is only realised at the rent reviews. For example in year 6, the calculation for the rent paid is 240,000*1.1^2*1.025^3.

12. Initial rent free period of 3 months.

13. Tenants' compensation under the Landlord and Tenants Act 1954 is based upon twice the rateable value on the assumption that there has been continued occupation of the existing premises for more than 14 years.

14. Timing of cash flows: all cash flows are to the midpoint of the year.

15. Decanting costs have not been included for option 1 for the sake of simplicity.

16. Costs of holding Crown Building vacant rent and running costs until lease expiry. Rent passing £200,000. Running costs when vacant £100,000

17. Costs of fitout/telecoms/removals to move to Crown Buildings estimated at £750,000

18. The costs of holding Crown Buildings vacant must be shown in Options 1 and 2 as the investment appraisal must account for all costs, not just to the individual Department

Annex 3: Land and Buildings

Land and Buildings Worked Example: Table 2
COST AND BENEFIT ANALYSIS

		Year	0	1	2	3	4	5	6	7	8	9	10	11	12	13	14	15
	Option 2 New City Centre Block																	
	Costs		-370	-796	-848	-841	-834	-828	-613	-610	-607	-605	-602	-632	-629	-627	-625	-873
	Additional Benefits																	
1	Improved disabled access			10	10	10	10	10	10	10	10	10	10	10	10	10	10	10
2	Reducing commuting time (visitors)			30	30	30	30	30	30	30	30	30	30	30	30	30	30	30
	Net cost		-370	-756	-808	-801	-794	-788	-573	-570	-567	-565	-562	-592	-589	-587	-585	-833
3	NPV(3.5%)	-8,225	-370	-743	-767	-735	-704	-675	-474	-456	-438	-421	-406	-413	-397	-382	-368	-506
	Option 3 Reuse Crown Building																	
	Costs		-870	-500	-498	-496	-494	-492	-543	-541	-538	-536	-534	-559	-113	-121	-130	-389
	Additional Benefits																	
	Improved disabled access			10	10	10	10	10	10	10	10	10	10	10	10	10	10	10
	Reducing commuting time (visitors)			30	30	30	30	30	30	30	30	30	30	30	30	30	30	30
	Net cost		-870	-460	-458	-456	-454	-452	-503	-501	-498	-496	-494	-519	-73	-81	-90	-349
	NPV (3.5%)	-5,625	-870	-452	-435	-418	-402	-387	-417	-400	-385	-370	-356	-361	-49	-53	-57	-212

NOTES TO TABLE 2

1 Calculated assuming that additional value is attached to these benefits.

2 Assumes that it is a public building.

3 Standard NPV calculation.

THE GREEN BOOK 77

Annex 3: Land and Buildings

RISK AND UNCERTAINTY

ANNEX 4

INTRODUCTION

1   This annex provides further guidance in each of the following areas:

- ❑ Risk management;
- ❑ Transferring risk;
- ❑ Optimism bias;
- ❑ Monte Carlo analysis;
- ❑ Irreversibility; and,
- ❑ The cost of variability in outcomes.

RISK MANAGEMENT

2   Risk management is a structured approach to identifying, assessing and controlling risks that emerge during the course of the policy, programme or project lifecycle. Its purpose is to support better decision-making through understanding the risks inherent in a proposal and their likely impact.

3   Effective risk management helps the achievement of wider aims, such as: effective change management; the efficient use of resources; better project management; minimising waste and fraud; and supporting innovation.

Organisation level risk management

4   Public sector organisations should foster a pragmatic approach to risk management at all levels.[1] This involves:

- ❑ Establishing a risk management framework, within which risks are identified and managed;
- ❑ Senior management support, ownership and leadership of risk management policies;
- ❑ Clear communication of organisational risk management policies to all staff; and
- ❑ Fully embedding risk management into business processes and ensuring it applies consistently.

5   These actions should help establish an organisational culture that supports well thought out risk taking and innovation.

Policy, programme and project level risk management

6   At the level of individual policies, programmes and policies, risk management strategies should be adopted in a way that is appropriate to their scale.

---

[1] On the 20 Novemeber 2002, the government (Strategy Unit) published new proposals to help improve risk management in the public sector. See the Cabinet Office website for further details (http://www.cabinet-office.gov.uk/)

Annex 4: Risk and Uncertainty

7   A risk register or risk log is a useful tool to identify, quantify and value the extent of risk and uncertainty relating to a proposal. A risk register / log can be used to identify the bearer of each risk and uncertainty associated with the project being appraised, provide an assessment of the likelihood of each risk occurring, and estimate its impact on project outcomes. Box 4.1 provides more detail.

BOX 4.1: RISK REGISTER (RISK LOG)

PURPOSE

A risk register lists all the identified risks and the results of their analysis and evaluation. Information on the status of the risk is also included. The risk register should be continuously updated and reviewed throughout the course of a project.

CONTENT

A risk register is best presented as a table for ease of reference and should contain the following information:

- Risk number (unique within register);
- Risk type;
- Author (who raised it);
- Date identified;
- Date last updated;
- Description;
- Likelihood;
- Interdependencies with other sources of risk;
- Expected impact;
- Bearer of risk;
- Countermeasures; and
- Risk status and risk action status.

FURTHER INFORMATION

For an example of a risk log and further information on the identification of risks and successful project and risk management refer to the OGC.[2]

Risk Mitigation

8   There are a number of approaches appraisers might take to mitigate the impact of the identified risks. These are outlined in Box 4.2.

---
[2] See website: http://www.ogc.gov.uk

BOX 4.2: OPTIONS TO HELP MANAGE RISK

- **Active risk management** – Effective management of risks involves:
  - identifying possible risks in advance and putting mechanisms in place to minimise the likelihood of their materialising with adverse effects;
  - having processes in place to monitor risks, and access to reliable, up-to-date information about risks;
  - the right balance of control in place to mitigate the adverse consequences of the risks, if they should materialise; and,
  - decision-making processes supported by a framework of risk analysis and evaluation.
- **Early consultation** – Experience suggests that costs tend to increase as more requirements are identified. Early consultation will help to identify what those needs are and how they may be addressed.
- **Avoidance of irreversible decisions** – Where lead options involve irreversibility, a full assessment of costs should include the possibility of delay, allowing more time for investigation of alternative ways to achieve the objectives.
- **Pilot Studies** – Acquiring more information about risks affecting a project through pilots allows steps to be taken to mitigate either the adverse consequences of bad outcomes, or increase the benefits of good outcomes.
- **Design Flexibility** – Where future demand and relative prices are uncertain, it may be worth choosing a flexible design adaptable to future changes, rather than a design suited to only one particular outcome. For example, different types of fuel can be used to fire a dual fired boiler, depending on future relative prices of alternative fuels. Breaking a project into stages, with successive review points at which the project could be stopped or changed, can also increase flexibility.
- **Precautionary Principle** – Precautionary action can be taken to mitigate a perceived risk. The precautionary principle states that because some outcomes are so bad, even though they may be very unlikely, precautionary action is justified. In cases where such risks have been identified, they should be drawn to the attention of senior management and expert advice sought.
- **Procurement / contractual** – risk can be contractually transferred to other parties and maintained through good contractual relationships, both formal and informal. Insurance is the most obvious example of risk transfer. The main text of this annex provides further information about the types of risk that can, and often are, transferred.
- **Making less use of leading edge technology** – If complex technology is involved, alternative, simpler methods should also be considered, especially if these reduce risk considerably whilst providing many of the benefits of the option involving leading edge technology.
- **Reinstate, or develop different options** – Following the risk analysis, the appraiser may want to reinstate or options, or develop alternative ones that are either less inherently risky or deal with the risks more efficiently.
- **Abandon proposal** – Finally, the proposal may be so risky that, whatever option is considered, it has to be abandoned.

Annex 4: Risk and Uncertainty

9   By reducing risks and uncertainty in these ways, the expected costs of a proposal are lowered or the expected benefits increased.

10   Additional guidance on risk management can be obtained from Risk Analysis and Management for Projects (RAMP), the Office of Government Commerce (OGC), the National Audit Office (NAO), HM Treasury, and the Cabinet Office.[3]

TRANSFERRING RISK

11   Box 4.3 describes the general types of risk a project manager is likely to encounter.[4]

12   Risk assessment will inform an overall view of the viability of an option, i.e. whether its risk-adjusted benefits exceed its risk-adjusted costs, or whether (in the case of uncertainty) the costs of a possible adverse outcome are so great that precautionary action needs to be introduced to obtain a cost-effective solution.

BOX 4.3: GENERAL TYPES OF RISK

Availability risk	The risk that the quantum of the service provided is less than that required under a contract.
Business risk	The risk that an organisation cannot meet its business imperatives.
Construction risk	The risk that the construction of physical assets is not completed on time, to budget and to specification.
Decant risk	The risk arising in accommodation projects relating to the need to decant staff/ clients from one site to another.
Demand risk	The risk that demand for a service does not match the levels planned, projected or assumed. As the demand for a service may be partially controllable by the public body concerned, the risk to the public sector may be less than that perceived by the private sector.
Design risk	The risk that design cannot deliver the services at the required performance or quality standards.
Economic risk	Where the project outcomes are sensitive to economic influences. For example, where actual inflation differs from assumed inflation rates.
Environment risk	Where the nature of the project has a major impact on its adjacent area and there is a strong likelihood of objection from the general public.

---

[3] Reference can be made to RAMP (http://www.ramprisk.com/), or the OGC (http://www.ogc.gov.uk/) for a range of materials including 'Managing a Successful Programme', HM Treasury: Management of Risk: A Strategic Overview (The 'Orange Book'), NAO: Supporting Innovation: Managing Risk in Government Departments. Also available are: Management of Risk: A Practitioner's Guide, published through the Stationery Office, and the Risk Portal found on the Cabinet Office website (http://www.cabinet-office.gov.uk/)

[4] See OGC website: http://www.ogc.gov.uk/

BOX 4.3: GENERAL TYPES OF RISK (contd)

Funding risk	Where project delays or changes in scope occur as a result of the availability of funding.
Legislative risk	The risk that changes in legislation increase costs. This can be sub-divided into general risks such as changes in corporate tax rates and specific ones which may affect a particular project.
Maintenance risk	The risk that the costs of keeping the assets in good condition vary from budget.
Occupancy risk	The risk that a property will remain untenanted – a form of demand risk.
Operational risk	The risk that operating costs vary from budget, that performance standards slip or that service cannot be provided.
Planning risk	The risk that the implementation of a project fails to adhere to the terms of planning permission or that detailed planning cannot be obtained, or if obtained, can only be implemented at costs greater than in the original budget.
Policy risk	The risk of changes of policy direction not involving legislation.
Procurement risk	Where a contractor is engaged, risk can arise from the contract between the two parties, the capabilities of the contractor, and when a dispute occurs.
Project intelligence risk	Where the quality of initial project intelligence (eg preliminary site investigation) is likely to impact on the likelihood of unforeseen problems occurring.
Reputational Risk	The risk that there, will be an undermining of customer/ media perception of the organisations ability to fulfil its business requirements e.g. adverse publicity concerning an operational problem.
Residual Value risk	The risk relating to the uncertainty of the value of physical assets at the end of the contract.
Technology risk	The risk that changes in technology result in services being provided using non-optimal technology.
Volume risk	The risk that actual usage of the service varies from the level forecast.

13   When faced with significant risks, a public body should consider transferring part or all of it to the private sector. The governing principle is that risk should be allocated to whichever party from the public or private sector is best placed to manage it. The optimal allocation of risk, rather than maximising risk transfer, is the objective, and is vital to ensuring that the best solution is found. Accordingly, the degree to which risk is transferred depends upon the specific proposal being appraised.

Annex 4: Risk and Uncertainty

14 Successful negotiation of risk transfer requires a clear understanding by the procuring authority of the risks presented by a proposal, the broad impact that these risks may have on the suppliers' incentives and financing costs, and the limits to risk transfer which might still be considered for value for money.

15 Where the private sector has clear ownership, responsibility and control, it should be encouraged to take all of those risks it can manage more effectively than the procuring authority. If the public body seeks to reserve many of the responsibilities and controls that go hand-in-hand with service delivery and yet still seek to transfer significant risk, there is a danger that the private sector will increase its prices.

16 Appropriate transfer of risk generates incentives for the private sector to supply timely cost effective and more innovative solutions. As a general rule, PFI schemes should transfer risks to the private sector when the supplier is better able to influence the outcome than the procuring authority. Risks to be considered include:

- Design and construction risk: to cost and/ or time;
- Technology and obsolescence risks;
- Commissioning and operating risks, including maintenance;
- Regulation and similar risks (including taxation, planning permission);
- Demand (or volume/ usage) risks;
- Residual value risk; and
- Project financing risk.

17 A risk allocation table can be a useful tool to identify the bearer of each risk relevant to a proposal. An example of this is set out in Box 4.4.

BOX 4.4: EXAMPLE OF RISK ALLOCATION TABLE

Risk	Scale	Bearer Purchaser	Bearer Provider	Key Issues
Obsolescence	Low		√	Assets require low levels of technology
Demand Risk	Med	√		…
Design risk	High		√	…
Residual Value	Low	√		…
3rd party revenues	Low		√	…
Regulatory change	High	√		…
etc.	…	…	…	…

Optimism Bias

18 Optimism bias is the demonstrated systematic tendency for appraisers to be over-optimistic about key project parameters. It must be accounted for explicitly in all appraisals, and can arise in relation to:

- Capital costs;
- Works duration;
- Operating costs; and
- Under delivery of benefits.

Capital costs

19 The two main causes of optimism bias in estimates of capital costs are:

- poor definition of the scope and objectives of projects in the business case, due to poor identification of stakeholder requirements, resulting in the omission of costs during project costing; and
- poor management of projects during implementation, so that schedules are not adhered to and risks are not mitigated.

20 Appraisers should adjust for optimism bias in the estimates of capital costs in the following way:

- Estimate the capital costs of each option;
- Apply adjustments to these estimates, based on the best available empirical evidence relevant to the stage of the appraisal; and,
- Subsequently, reduce these adjustments according to the extent of confidence in the capital costs' estimates, the extent of management of generic risks, and the extent of work undertaken to identify and mitigate project specific risks.

21 Departments or agencies may be able to provide the best empirical evidence to support adjustments for optimism. Alternatively, and if applicable, they may be taken from the Green Book homepage[5], which provides the recommended adjustments to be made at the outline business case stage for buildings, civil engineering, equipment and development, and outsourcing projects.

22 If no obvious empirical evidence is available, this may indicate that the project is unique or unusual, in which case optimism bias is likely to be high. In these cases, adjustments should be based on the nearest equivalent project type, and adjusted up or down, depending on how inherently risky the project is compared to its nearest equivalent type.

23 If a department chooses to apply its own adjustments, these must be prudent. Where possible, the cost estimates, and the adjustments for optimism bias should be reviewed externally (using Gateway reviews for large projects, or internal audit reviews of smaller projects).

---

[6] See website: http://www.hm-treasury.gov.uk/greenbook for empirical adjustments for generic project categories outlined in Review of Large Public Procurement in the UK, published in July 2002

Annex 4: Risk and Uncertainty

Works duration

24 The same approach should be taken with estimating the length of time it will take to complete the capital works. In summary:

- Estimate the time taken to complete the capital works;

- Apply adjustments to these estimates, based on the best available empirical evidence relevant to the stage of the appraisal;

- Subsequently, reduce these adjustments according to the extent of confidence in the works duration estimates, the extent of management of generic risks, and the extent of work undertaken to identify and mitigate project specific risks; and,

- The estimates of works' duration, and the adjustments for optimism, should ideally be reviewed independently.

25 The application of optimism bias adjustments to works' duration should be reflected in a delay in the receipt of benefits. This will be shown in the net present value calculations. The appraisal period may need to be extended to reflect the expected delay in benefits' stream, but different periods should not usually be set for different options.

Operating costs and benefits

26 Analysis should also be undertaken on potential benefits' shortfalls and increases in operating costs. If there is no evidence to support adjustments to operating costs or benefits' shortfalls, appraisers should use sensitivity analysis. This should help to answer key questions such as:

- By how much can we allow benefits to fall short of expectations, if the proposal is to remain worthwhile? How likely is this?

- How much can operating costs increase, if the proposal is to remain worthwhile? How likely is this to happen?

- What will be the impact on benefits if operating costs are constrained?

Preventing optimism bias

27 To minimise the level of optimism bias in appraisal, best practice[6] suggests that the following actions should be taken:

- Project managers, suitably competent and experienced for the role, should be identified;

- Project sponsor roles should be clearly defined;

- Recognised project management structures should be in place;

- Performance management systems should be set up; and

---

[6] 'Review of Large Public Procurement in the UK', Mott MacDonald (2002), available at www.hm-treasury.gov.uk/greenbook

Annex 4: Risk and Uncertainty

- For large or complex projects:
    - Simpler alternatives should be developed wherever possible;
    - Consideration should be given to breaking down large, ambitious projects into smaller ones with more easily defined and achievable goals; and,
    - Knowledge transfer processes should be set up, so that changes in individual personnel do not disrupt the smooth implementation of a project.

MONTE CARLO ANALYSIS

28 Monte Carlo analysis allows an assessment of the consequences of simultaneous uncertainty about key inputs, and can take account of correlations between these inputs. It involves replacing single entries with probability distributions of possible values for key inputs. Typically, the choice of probabilistic inputs will be based on prior sensitivity testing. The calculation is then repeated a large number of times randomly (using a computer program) to combine different input values selected from the probability distributions specified. The results consist of a set of probability distributions showing how uncertainties in key inputs might impact on key outcomes.

29 Box 4.5 provides an example illustrating the use of Monte Carlo analysis.[1]

BOX 4.5: ALLOWING FOR UNCERTAINTY IN AN ANALYSIS OF COSTS

The table below gives the costs of various parts of a construction project, broken down into excavation (E), foundations (F), structure (S), roofing (R), and decorations (D). All costs are independent of each other. The model for total cost is as follows:

Total cost = E + F + S + R + D

Costs for construction project (£)

	Minimum	Best Guess	Maximum
Excavation (E)	30,500	33,200	37,800
Foundations (F)	23,500	27,200	31,100
Structure (S)	172,000	178,000	189,000
Roofing (R)	56,200	58,500	63,700
Decoration (D)	29,600	37,200	43,600

From this information we can produce a best guess of £334,100 for the total cost of the project. However, we can also conclude a possible range from £311,800 to £365,200. Suppose the project would not go ahead unless the total cost is unlikely to exceed £350,000; how much assurance can we take from these figures that the total cost will be less than £350,000?

---

[1] This example was adapted from 'Measuring costs and benefits – a guide on cost benefit and cost effectiveness analysis', National Audit Office (NAO) and Vose, D (1996)

Annex 4: Risk and Uncertainty

> **BOX 4.5: ALLOWING FOR UNCERTAINTY IN AN ANALYSIS OF COSTS (contd)**
>
> By undertaking a Monte Carlo analysis, we can simulate many possible values of the input variables, weighted so that the 'best guess' value is more likely than the extreme values. The total cost is calculated for each simulation, giving a distribution of values for total cost. The precise weighting depends on the probability distributions specified for each variable.
>
> Using triangular distributions, it can be concluded that the most likely total cost is £334,000; and that the chance of total cost exceeding £350,000 is less than 1%.

IRREVERSIBLE RISK

30 Irreversibility occurs where implementation of a proposal might rule out later investment opportunities or alternative uses of resources. Examples of irreversibility are destruction of natural environments or historic buildings. It is particularly important to make a full assessment of the costs of any irreversible damage that may arise from a proposal.

31 Irreversibility is often associated with facilities on which people place 'option values' (the value of knowing a facility is available to enjoy, if they wish to do so). This is also linked to 'existence values' (the value of knowing that something continues to exist, even if the respondent does not expect to make any practical use of it).

32 Where lead options involve irreversible damage, assessment should include the consideration of options which involve delay, allowing more time for investigation of alternative less damaging ways to achieve stated objectives. Appraisal of different proposals should not ignore the 'option' value of avoiding or delaying irreversible actions, and the benefits of ensuring flexibility to respond to future changed conditions.

THE COST OF VARIABILITY IN OUTCOMES

33 In estimating the future costs and benefits associated with particular proposals, there will inevitably be variation between these estimates and the actual costs and benefits realised. This will be over and above the impact of optimism bias, and will be as a result of random factors unforeseen at the time of appraisal.

34 For the public sector as a whole, such random factors will tend to cancel out, taking all proposals together. But in some cases, this would not be expected to happen. Some projects - for example transport use - will tend to have appraisal risks that are systematically related to the overall performance of the economy. Because the majority or all of such projects will be affected by this same factor, appraisal errors will not cancel out between projects.

35 A decision-maker who is risk averse cares about this potential variability in outcomes, and is willing to pay a sum in exchange for certainty (or willing to put up with variability on receipt of compensation). This compensation is the cost of variability, and should be included in appraisal when it is considered appropriate.

36 Generally, a variability adjustment may be required when:

- ❑ Risks are large relative to the income of the section of the population that must bear them (including very large risks borne by the whole population); or

THE GREEN BOOK

Annex 4: Risk and Uncertainty

❏ When risk is correlated systematically with income or GDP, and so cannot be diluted by spreading across the economy.

37 The fraction of income worth paying for certainty (C) is approximated by the expression:

$$C = - var(y) / 2y^*$$

where y is the net additional income resulting from the proposal, and y^* is the total expected income or benefits (including the project income) of those impacted by the proposal.

38 Given the size of national income relative to the scale of most individual projects, the cost of variability for projects that benefit the community as a whole is usually negligible.

Annex 4: Risk and Uncertainty

Distributional Impacts

Annex 5

Introduction

1   'Distributional impacts' is a term used to describe the distribution of the costs or benefits of interventions across different groups in society. Proposals might have differential impacts on individuals, amongst other aspects, according to their:

- Income;
- Gender;
- Ethnic group;
- Age;
- Geographical location; or
- Disability.

2   It is important that these distributional issues are assessed in appraisals.

Distributional Analysis

3   Any distributional effects identified should be explicitly stated and quantified as far as possible. At a minimum, this requires appraisers to identify how the costs and benefits accrue to different groups in society. If, for example, the costs of a government action fall largely upon one ethnic group this impact should be detailed in the appraisal.

4   It follows from this that a rigorous analysis of how the costs and benefits of a proposal are spread across different socio-economic groups is recommended. Where it is considered necessary and practical, this might involve explicitly recognising distributional effects within a project's NPV.

Analysis of Impacts according to Relative Prosperity

5   The impact of a proposal on an individual's well-being will vary according to income; as income grows, the satisfaction derived from an additional unit of consumption declines.

6   The relative prosperity of a household affected by a proposal is determined not only by its income, but also by its size and composition. For example, a single person on £100 a week is better off than a couple on £100 a week. Table 5.1 adjusts for varying costs of living for some specimen family types through a process called equivalisation. These calculations use the McClements scale[1] that takes account of the number of adults and the number and ages of children in the household.

---

[1] DWP, Households Below Average Income, (2000/01)

THE GREEN BOOK

Annex 5: Distributional Impacts

TABLE 5.1: INCOME RANGES BY QUINTILE OF EQUIVALISED NET INCOME

£ per week	Single with no children	Couple with no children	Single with child aged 5-7	Couple with child aged 5-7	Single with two children aged 5 & 11	Couple with two children aged 5 & 11	Single with Pensioner	Pensioner Couple
Quintile of equivalised net income								
1	0 to 114	0 to 184	0 to 154	0 to 224	0 to 199	0 to 269	0 to 114	0 to 184
2	115 to 154	185 to 254	155 to 209	225 to 309	200 to 274	270 to 369	115 to 154	185 to 254
3	155 to 204	255 to 339	210 to 274	310 to 409	275 to 359	370 to 494	155 to 204	255 to 339
4	205 to 284	340 to 469	275 to 384	410 to 564	360 to 499	495 to 684	205 to 284	340 to 469
5	285 plus	470 plus	385 plus	565 plus	500 plus	685 plus	285 plus	470 plus

Table 5.2 provides the same rankings for specimen family types in terms of equivalised gross income.

TABLE 5.2: INCOME RANGES BY QUINTILE OF EQUIVALISED GROSS INCOME

£ per week	Single with no children	Couple with no children	Single with child aged 5-7	Couple with child aged 5-7	Single with two children aged 5 & 11	Couple with two children aged 5 & 11	Single with Pensioner	Pensioner Couple
Quintile of equivalised gross income								
1	0 to 129	0 to 214	0 to 174	0 to 259	0 to 224	0 to 309	0 to 129	0 to 214
2	130 to 89	215 to 314	175 to 254	260 379	225 to 334	310 to 459	130 to 189	215 to 314
3	190 to 269	315 to 444	255 to 364	380 to 534	335 to 474	460 to 644	190 to 269	315 to 444
4	270 to 394	445 to 644	265 to 529	535 to 779	475 to 689	645 to 939	270 to 394	445 to 644
5	395 plus	645 plus	530 plus	780 plus	690 plus	940 plus	395 plus	645 plus

7 Appraisers should assess how the costs and benefits of each option are spread across different income groups, such as the income quintiles provided in Table 5.1 or Table 5.2.[2] A proposal providing greater net benefits to lower income quintiles is rated more favourably than one whose benefits largely accrue to higher quintiles.

8 Further analysis can then be undertaken, using distributional weights, to recognise the identified impacts within the cost-benefit analysis. A benefit or cost accruing to a relatively low income family would be weighted more heavily than one accruing to a high income family.

9 In principle, each **monetary** cost and benefit should be weighted according to the relative prosperity of those receiving the benefit or bearing the cost.[3] However, in practice, this information is most unlikely to be available at acceptable cost for many applications. The decision on whether an explicit adjustment is warranted should be informed by the:

---

[2] Where a household being assessed is not defined by one of the categories in Table 5.1 or Table 5.2, appraisers should use the closest specimen family.

[3] Generally, non-monetary costs and benefits (eg life, health, time savings, etc) are not adjusted as they are considered to be independent of income. For example, the DfT's valuation of non-working travel time savings is averaged across all income groups, so has already been implicitly equity weighted. If values are not standard and are calculated for a specific project an adjustment might still be required.

THE GREEN BOOK

Annex 5: Distributional Impacts

- Scale of the impact associated with a particular project or proposal;
- Likely robustness of any calculation of distributional impacts; and,
- The type of project being assessed.

10   If appraisers decide not to use distributional weights to make an explicit adjustment, this decision must be fully justified.

Deriving distributional weights

11   One approach to deriving the weights used is the concept of an underlying social welfare function that links personal utility (or satisfaction) to income.

12   Broadly, the empirical evidence suggests that as income is doubled, the marginal value of consumption to individuals is halved: the utility of a marginal pound is inversely proportional to the income of the recipient. In other words, an extra £1 of consumption received by someone earning £10,000 a year will be worth twice as much as when it is paid to a person earning £20,000 per annum.

BOX 5.1: THE MARGINAL UTILITY OF CONSUMPTION

Welfare Weights, by Cowell and Gardiner (1999) concluded that "most [studies] imply values of the elasticity of marginal utility of just below or just above one".[4] Pearce and Ulph (1995), in their survey of the evidence, estimate a range from 0.7 to 1.5, with a value of 1 being defensible.[5]

Assuming a value of 1 implies a utility function of the form

$$U = \log C$$

where C is consumption.

The marginal utility of consumption is then given by $\delta U/\delta C$ i.e. $1/C$.

This implies that if consumption doubles, the marginal utility of consumption falls to one half of the previous value.

13   Box 5.2 provides an example of how distributional weights might be calculated from the equivalised income quintiles in Table 5.1 or Table 5.2. The weights provided are merely illustrative. Despite this uncertainty it is important that appraisers, where deemed appropriate, attempt to adjust explicitly for distributional implications. The assumptions underpinning the chosen distributional weights should be fully explained.

---

[4] Cowell and Gardiner (1999) page 31

[5] Pearce and Ulph (1995) page 14

Annex 5: Distributional Impacts

BOX 5.2: DERIVING ILLUSTRATIVE DISTRIBUTIONAL WEIGHTS

The marginal utility of each quintile in Tables 5.1 and 5.2 can be calculated by dividing 1 by the median income of each quintile ($U' = 1/C$). Distributional weights can then be derived by expressing the marginal utility of each quintile as a percentage of average marginal utility (1 divided by the median income). The table below provides the illustrative weights as ranges, reflecting uncertainty in the utility function and the assumed income quintiles.

Quintile	Range (Net)	Range (Gross)
Bottom	1.9 – 2.0	2.2 – 2.3
2nd	1.3 – 1.4	1.4 – 1.5
3rd	0.9 – 1.0	1.0 – 1.1
4th	0.7 – 0.8	0.7 – 0.8
Top	0.4 – 0.5	0.4 – 0.5

14   It will often be the case that neither net nor gross incomes of those affected by a proposal are known directly, so as to allow the distributional adjustment to be calculated. However, if the family or other circumstances of a group affected are known, an adjustment may be calculable indirectly using whatever is known about the relative incomes of those in the relevant category.

15   For example, it may be that a particular proposal will disproportionately provide additional employment for people on probation in a particular area. If it is known that probationers in that area are predominantly in the lowest income quintile, it will be reasonable to use the adjustment factor calculated for that quintile.

16   The regional impact of policy may assist the analysis: the income impact of a proposal may be estimated indirectly by determining its geographical impact and taking note of small-area indices of deprivation.[6] However, care must be taken to assess whether the beneficiaries of a proposal are representative of the geographical area from which they come.

ANALYSIS OF OTHER DISTRIBUTIONAL IMPACTS

17   UK discrimination law currently covers gender, marriage, disability and race. In addition, the government is bound by European law, which currently covers discrimination on the grounds of gender, marital status, pregnancy and maternity only, but is likely to be extended in due course.

18   The scope of racial discrimination law in the UK has recently been significantly extended with the Race Relations (Amendment) Act 2000. It now requires certain listed public authorities to comply with a new general duty to promote racial equality.[7] This aims to ensure that the listed bodies give due regard to racial equality when carrying out their functions, including policy-making.

---

[6] 'Where does public spending go? A pilot study to analyse the flows of public expenditures into local areas', by the former DETR (now ODPM).

[7] See Section 71 of the Race Relations Act 1976 (as amended by the Race Relations (Amendment) Act 2000)

Annex 5: Distributional Impacts

19   The UK is also a signatory to various international treaties and conventions with anti discrimination provisions. These do not provide the right of individual complaint against the UK, but should inform the development of policy. Box 5.3 details the relevant legislation and the more important conventions.

BOX 5.3: RELEVANT ANTI DISCRIMINATION LEGISLATION, TREATIES AND CONVENTIONS

ANTI DISCRIMINATION LEGISLATION
- The Sex Discrimination Act 1975 (as amended)
- The Employment Act 1989 & The Employment Rights Act 1996
- The Equal Pay Act 1970 (as amended)
- The Race Relations Act 1976 (as amended)
- The Disability Discrimination Act (1995)
- Pregnant Workers Directive
- Article 119 of the Treaty of Rome, and Equal Treatment and Equal Pay Directives made under the Treaty. EC Law on free movement of workers, services and capital, and freedom of establishment.

CONVENTIONS
- The UN Convention on the Elimination of All Forms of Discrimination against Women
- The UN Convention on the Elimination of All Forms of Racial Discrimination
- The UN International Covenant on Civil & Political Rights
- The UN International Covenant on Economic, Social and Cultural Rights
- The UN Standard Rules on Equalisation of Opportunities for People with Disabilities
- The Council of Europe European Convention on Human Rights

20   Analysis of distributional issues should not be limited to assessing compliance with discrimination law, and international treaties and conventions. Unless appraisers consider the impact a particular proposal has on different groups in society, they cannot be sure the action is having the intended affect.

21   There are three steps when considering equality during appraisal[8]:

1. Analyse how the proposal will affect different groups of people (e.g. gender, ethnic group, age, disabled, location).

2. Consider whether there are any adverse differential impacts on a particular group. If so, are these impacts unfair or unlawful, or do they contradict overall Government policy.

---
[8] See Policy Appraisal for Equal Treatment, issued to all departments in 1998 by the Cabinet Office, Home Office, and the (then) DfEE

THE GREEN BOOK

3. If the action is not permissible in the above senses, remedial action is necessary. If, however, it is permissible, appraisers must decide:

- If alternative action could meet the objectives without the same adverse consequences; or
- Whether there are any measures that can be taken to reduce the predicted adverse impact.

22 Following is a list of useful organisations when considering equality in appraisal:

- Equal Opportunities Commission (EOC)
- Commission for Racial Equality (CRE)
- Women and Equality Unit – Cabinet Office
- Race and Gender Mainstreaming Team – Home Office
- Disability Rights Commission

Discount Rate

Annex 6

Introduction

1 This Annex shows how the discount rate of 3.5 per cent real is derived and the circumstances in which it should be applied.

Social Time Preference Rate

2 Social Time Preference is defined as the value society attaches to present, as opposed to future, consumption. The Social Time Preference Rate (STPR) is a rate used for discounting future benefits and costs, and is based on comparisons of utility across different points in time or different generations. This guidance recommends that the STPR be used as the standard real discount rate.

3 The STPR has two components:

- ❑ The rate at which individuals discount future consumption over present consumption, on the assumption that no change in per capita consumption is expected, represented by ρ; and,

- ❑ An additional element, if per capita consumption is expected to grow over time, reflecting the fact that these circumstances imply future consumption will be plentiful relative to the current position and thus have lower marginal utility. This effect is represented by the product of the annual growth in per capita consumption (g) and the elasticity of marginal utility of consumption (μ) with respect to utility.

The STPR, represented by r, is the sum of these two components, i.e.

$$r = \rho + \mu.g \qquad (1)$$

Each element of STPR is examined in turn below.

Estimates of ρ

4 This comprises two elements:

- ❑ Catastrophe risk (L); and
- ❑ Pure time preference (δ).

5 The first component, catastrophe risk, is the likelihood that there will be some event so devastating that all returns from policies, programmes or projects are eliminated, or at least radically and unpredictably altered. Examples are technological advancements that lead to premature obsolescence, or natural disasters, major wars etc. The scale of this risk is, by its nature, hard to quantify.[1]

6 The second component, pure time preference, reflects individuals' preference for consumption now, rather than later, with an unchanging level of consumption per capita over time.[2]

---

[1] Newbery (1992) estimates L as 1.0, Kula (1987) as 1.2, Pearce and Ulph (1995) as 1.2, OXERA (2002) as 1.1 currently and 1 in the near future.

[2] Scott (1977, 1989) estimates δ as 0.5. Other literature suggests it lies between 0.0 and 0.5. However, if zero, this implies pure time preference does not exist, which is not regarded as plausible.

Annex 6: Discount Rate

7 The evidence suggests that these two components indicate a value for ρ of around 1.5 per cent a year for the near future.[3]

Estimates of μ

8 The available evidence suggests the elasticity of the marginal utility of consumption (μ) is around 1.[4] This implies that a marginal increment in consumption to a generation that has twice the consumption of the current generation will reduce the utility by half.

Estimates of g

9 Maddison (2001) shows growth per capita in UK to be 2.1 per cent over the period 1950 to 1998. Surveying the evidence, the Treasury paper *Trend Growth: Recent Developments and Prospects* also suggests a figure of 2.1 per cent for output growth to be reasonable.[5] The annual rate of g is therefore put at 2 per cent per year.

The calculated STPR

So with g = 2 per cent, ρ = 1.5 per cent, μ = 1.0, then from equation (1) the STPR to be used as the real discount rate is

$$0.015 + 1.0 * 0.02 = \mathbf{3.5 \text{ per cent}}$$

LONG-TERM DISCOUNT RATES

10 Where the appraisal of a proposal depends materially upon the discounting of effects in the very long term, the received view is that a lower discount rate for the longer term (beyond 30 years) should be used.[6]

11 The main rationale for declining long-term discount rates results from uncertainty about the future. This uncertainty can be shown to cause declining discount rates over time.[7]

12 In light of this evidence, it is recommended that for costs and benefits accruing more than 30 years into the future, appraisers use the schedule of discount rates provided in Table 6.1 below.

---

[3] Scott (1977) derives a central estimate value of 1.5 from past long-term returns received by savers in the UK. A later estimate in Scott (1989), updated this estimate to 1.3. However, this was based on United States, as well as UK, evidence. OXERA (2002) estimates ρ to lie between 1.0 and 1.6.

[4] Pearce and Ulph (1995) estimate a range from 0.7 to 1.5 with 1.0 being considered defensible; Cowell and Gardiner (1999) estimate μ as being just below or just above one; OXERA (2002) estimate a range from 0.8 to 1.1.

[5] This estimate removes the impact of net migration. The paper is available on the HM Treasury website (http://www.hm-treasury.gov.uk).

[6] OXERA (2002)

[7] Weitzman (1998, 2001) and Gollier (2002)

Annex 6: Discount Rate

TABLE 6.1: THE DECLINING LONG TERM DISCOUNT RATE

Period of years	0–30	31–75	76–125	126–200	201–300	301+
Discount rate	3.5%	3.0%	2.5%	2.0%	1.5%	1.0%

EXCEPTIONS TO THE DISCOUNT RATE SCHEDULE

13 The standard schedule of discount rates may not be appropriate in the following circumstances.

- For international development assistance projects, a discount rate derived from estimates of the social time preference rate appropriate to the recipient economy should be used.

- When undertaking sensitivity analysis, the impact of changing the precise value of the discount rate can be analysed in the same way as for other parameters in the appraisal. The rationale for undertaking sensitivity analysis on the discount rate should be clearly explained.

Annex 6: Discount Rate

DISCOUNT FACTORS

Year	1.0%	2.0%	3.0%	3.5%	4.0%	5.0%	6.0%	7.0%	8.0%	9.0%	10.0%
0	1.0000	1.0000	1.0000	1.0000	1.0000	1.0000	1.0000	1.0000	1.0000	1.0000	1.0000
1	0.9901	0.9804	0.9709	0.9662	0.9615	0.9524	0.9434	0.9346	0.9259	0.9174	0.9091
2	0.9803	0.9612	0.9426	0.9335	0.9246	0.9070	0.8900	0.8734	0.8573	0.8417	0.8264
3	0.9706	0.9423	0.9151	0.9019	0.8890	0.8638	0.8396	0.8163	0.7938	0.7722	0.7513
4	0.9610	0.9238	0.8885	0.8714	0.8548	0.8227	0.7921	0.7629	0.7350	0.7084	0.6830
5	0.9515	0.9057	0.8626	0.8420	0.8219	0.7835	0.7473	0.7130	0.6806	0.6499	0.6209
6	0.9420	0.8880	0.8375	0.8135	0.7903	0.7462	0.7050	0.6663	0.6302	0.5963	0.5645
7	0.9327	0.8706	0.8131	0.7860	0.7599	0.7107	0.6651	0.6227	0.5835	0.5470	0.5132
8	0.9235	0.8535	0.7894	0.7594	0.7307	0.6768	0.6274	0.5820	0.5403	0.5019	0.4665
9	0.9143	0.8368	0.7664	0.7337	0.7026	0.6446	0.5919	0.5439	0.5002	0.4604	0.4241
10	0.9053	0.8203	0.7441	0.7089	0.6756	0.6139	0.5584	0.5083	0.4632	0.4224	0.3855
11	0.8963	0.8043	0.7224	0.6849	0.6496	0.5847	0.5268	0.4751	0.4289	0.3875	0.3505
12	0.8874	0.7885	0.7014	0.6618	0.6246	0.5568	0.4970	0.4440	0.3971	0.3555	0.3186
13	0.8787	0.7730	0.6810	0.6394	0.6006	0.5303	0.4688	0.4150	0.3677	0.3262	0.2897
14	0.8700	0.7579	0.6611	0.6178	0.5775	0.5051	0.4423	0.3878	0.3405	0.2992	0.2633
15	0.8613	0.7430	0.6419	0.5969	0.5553	0.4810	0.4173	0.3624	0.3152	0.2745	0.2394
16	0.8528	0.7284	0.6232	0.5767	0.5339	0.4581	0.3936	0.3387	0.2919	0.2519	0.2176
17	0.8444	0.7142	0.6050	0.5572	0.5134	0.4363	0.3714	0.3166	0.2703	0.2311	0.1978
18	0.8360	0.7002	0.5874	0.5384	0.4936	0.4155	0.3503	0.2959	0.2502	0.2120	0.1799
19	0.8277	0.6864	0.5703	0.5202	0.4746	0.3957	0.3305	0.2765	0.2317	0.1945	0.1635
20	0.8195	0.6730	0.5537	0.5026	0.4564	0.3769	0.3118	0.2584	0.2145	0.1784	0.1486
21	0.8114	0.6598	0.5375	0.4856	0.4388	0.3589	0.2942	0.2415	0.1987	0.1637	0.1351
22	0.8034	0.6468	0.5219	0.4692	0.4220	0.3418	0.2775	0.2257	0.1839	0.1502	0.1228
23	0.7954	0.6342	0.5067	0.4533	0.4057	0.3256	0.2618	0.2109	0.1703	0.1378	0.1117
24	0.7876	0.6217	0.4919	0.4380	0.3901	0.3101	0.2470	0.1971	0.1577	0.1264	0.1015
25	0.7798	0.6095	0.4776	0.4231	0.3751	0.2953	0.2330	0.1842	0.1460	0.1160	0.0923
26	0.7720	0.5976	0.4637	0.4088	0.3607	0.2812	0.2198	0.1722	0.1352	0.1064	0.0839
27	0.7644	0.5859	0.4502	0.3950	0.3468	0.2678	0.2074	0.1609	0.1252	0.0976	0.0763
28	0.7568	0.5744	0.4371	0.3817	0.3335	0.2551	0.1956	0.1504	0.1159	0.0895	0.0693
29	0.7493	0.5631	0.4243	0.3687	0.3207	0.2429	0.1846	0.1406	0.1073	0.0822	0.0630
30	0.7419	0.5521	0.4120	0.3563	0.3083	0.2314	0.1741	0.1314	0.0994	0.0754	0.0573

LONG TERM DISCOUNT FACTORS

Year	Long Term Discount Factor	Year	Long Term Discount Factor
0	1.0000	23	0.4533
1	0.9662	24	0.4380
2	0.9335	25	0.4231
3	0.9019	26	0.4088
4	0.8714	27	0.3950
5	0.8420	28	0.3817
6	0.8135	29	0.3687
7	0.7860	30	0.3563
8	0.7594	40	0.2651
9	0.7337	50	0.1973
10	0.7089	60	0.1468
11	0.6849	75	0.0942
12	0.6618	80	0.0833
13	0.6394	90	0.0651
14	0.6178	100	0.0508
15	0.5969	125	0.0274
16	0.5767	150	0.0167
17	0.5572	200	0.0062
18	0.5384	250	0.0029
19	0.5202	300	0.0014
20	0.5026	350	0.0009
21	0.4856	400	0.0005
22	0.4692	500	0.0002

THE GREEN BOOK

Glossary

Additionality An impact arising from an intervention is additional if it would not have occurred in the absence of the intervention.

Adverse Selection When asymmetric information restricts the quality of the good traded. This typically happens because the person with more information is able to negotiate a favourable exchange.

Affordability An assessment of whether proposals can be paid for in terms of cashflows and resource costs.

Appraisal The process of defining objectives, examining options and weighing up the costs benefits, risks and uncertainties of those options before a decision is made.

Assessment(s) Either an appraisal or an evaluation (or both).

Base Case The best estimate of how much a proposal will cost in economic terms, including an allowance for risk and optimism.

Choice modelling This term encompasses a range of stated preference techniques and includes choice experiments (often preferred because of its firm base in welfare economics), contingent ranking, contingent rating and paired comparisons.

Contingent valuation This involves directly asking people how much they would be willing to pay for a good or service, or how much they are willing to accept to give it up.

Contingency An allowance of cash or resources to cover unforeseen circumstances.

Cost Benefit Analysis Analysis which quantifies in monetary terms as many of the costs and benefits of a proposal as feasible, including items for which the market does not provide a satisfactory measure of economic value.

Cost-Effectiveness Analysis Analysis that compares the costs of alternative ways of producing the same or similar outputs.

Cost of capital The cost of raising funds (expressed as an annual percentage rate).

Cost of variability in outcomes This is the most a person is willing to pay to have a benefit that is certain, rather than one that is uncertain.

Crowding out The extent to which an increase in demand occasioned by government policy is offset by a decrease in private sector demand.

Deadweight Expenditure to promote a desired activity that would in fact have occurred without the expenditure.

Diminishing marginal utility The tendency as extra units of any commodity or service are used up or 'consumed', for the satisfaction provided by those extra units to decline.

Discounting A method used to convert future costs or benefits to present values using a discount rate.

Glossary

Discounted Cash Flow (DCF) A technique for appraising investments. It reflects the principle that the value to an investor (whether an individual or a firm) of a sum of money depends on when it is received.

Discount rate The annual percentage rate at which the present value of a future pound, or other unit of account, is assumed to fall away through time.

Displacement The degree to which an increase in productive capacity promoted by government policy is offset by reductions in productive capacity elsewhere.

Do minimum option An option where government takes the minimum amount of action necessary.

Economic cost (or opportunity cost) The value of the most valuable of alternative uses.

Economic Efficiency This is achieved when nobody can be made better off without someone else being made worse off.

Effectiveness A measure of the extent to which a project, programme or policy achieves its objectives.

Evaluation Retrospective analysis of a project, programme, or policy to assess how successful or otherwise it has been, and what lessons can be learnt for the future. The terms 'policy evaluation' and 'post-project evaluation' are often used to describe evaluation in those two areas.

Existence value The value placed by people on the continued existence of an asset for the benefit of present or future generations. The latter is sometimes referred to as bequest value. See also Use value.

Expected value The weighted average of all possible values of a variable, where the weights are the probabilities.

Externality costs or benefits The non-market impacts of an intervention or activity which are not borne by those who generate them.

GDP deflator An index of the general price level in the economy as a whole, measured by the ratio of gross domestic product (GDP) in nominal (i.e. cash) terms to GDP at constant prices.

Hedonic pricing Deriving values by decomposing market prices into their constituent characteristics.

Information asymmetry Differences in information held by parties to a transaction where this information is relevant to determining an efficient contract or a fair price or for monitoring or rewarding performance.

Impact statement A description, quantified where possible, of all the significant impacts of a proposal, and of how they are distributed between those affected.

Implementation The activities required during the period after appraisal to put in place a policy, or complete a programme or project, at which point 'normal' service is achieved.

Internal rate of return (IRR) The discount rate that would give a project a present value of zero.

Glossary

Irreversibility This applies when an option would rule out later investment opportunities, or would use resources now that might subsequently be preferred for a more important later use.

Market failure An imperfection in the market mechanism that prevents the achievement of economic efficiency.

Market value The price at which a commodity can be bought or sold, determined through the interaction of buyers and sellers in a market.

Marginal utility The increase in satisfaction gained by a consumer from a small increase in the consumption of a good or service.

Monte Carlo analysis A technique that allows assessment of the consequences of simultaneous uncertainty about key inputs, taking account of correlations between these inputs.

Moral Hazard An example of information asymmetry where a contract or relationship places incentives upon one party to take (or not take) unobservable steps which are prejudicial to another party.

Multi Criteria Analysis See Weighting and Scoring

Net Present Value (NPV) The discounted value of a stream of either future costs or benefits. The term Net Present Value (NPV) is used to describe the difference between the present value of a stream of costs and a stream of benefits.

Opportunity cost (or Economic cost) The value of the most valuable of alternative uses.

Optimism bias The demonstrated systematic tendency for appraisers to be over-optimistic about key project parameters, including capital costs, operating costs, works duration and benefits delivery.

Option appraisal The appraisal of various options chosen to achieve specific objectives.

Option value The value of the availability of the option of using an environmental or other asset (which in this context is usually non-marketed) at some future date. See also Use value.

PFI Private Finance Initiative

PPP Public Private Partnership

Precautionary principle The concept that precautionary action can be taken to mitigate a perceived risk. Action may be justified even if the probability of that risk occurring is small, because the outcome might be very adverse.

Present Value The future value expressed in present terms by means of discounting

Price index A measure of the amount by which prices change over time. General price indexes cover a wide range of prices and include the GDP deflator and the Retail Price Index (RPI). Special price indices apply to one commodity or type of commodity.

Proposal An idea for a policy, programme or project that is under appraisal.

Glossary

Public Sector Comparator Public Sector Comparator is a hypothetical risk-adjusted costing, by the public sector as a supplier, to an output specification produced as part of a PFI procurement exercise. It:

- is expressed in net present value terms;

- is based on the recent actual public sector method of providing that defined output (including any reasonably foreseeable efficiencies the public sector could make); and,

- takes full account of the risks which would be encountered by that style of procurement.

Pure time preference Pure time preference is the preference for consumption now, rather than later.

Real option theory This presumes that decision making is sequential and that decision makers may benefit from choosing options that may seem sub optimal today but which increase flexibility at later times, leading to better decision making when more is known about the project.

Real price The nominal (i.e. cash) price deflated by a general price index, e.g. RPI or GDP deflator, relative to a specified base year or base date.

Real terms The value of expenditure at a specified general price level: that is a cash price or expenditure divided by a general price index.

Relative price effect The movement over time of a specific price index (such as construction prices) relative to a general price index (such as the GDP deflator).

Relevant cost/benefit All costs and benefits that can be affected by decisions and that are therefore related to the objectives and scope of the proposal in hand.

Required rate of return A target average rate of return for a public sector trading body, usually expressed, for central government bodies, as a return on the current cost value of total capital employed.

Resources/ resource cost Terms used in a variety of senses, according to context. In resource accounting, 'resource costs' are accruals accounting costs expressed in real terms. In economic analysis a distinction is sometimes drawn between 'transfers', such as social security payments and 'resource costs' which are payments for goods or services. In departments and agencies 'resources' is a term sometimes used to describe expenditure from their budgets, or sometimes requirements of staffing.

Revealed preference The inference of willingness to pay for something which is non-marketed by examining consumer behaviour in a similar or related market.

Risk The likelihood, measured by its probability, that a particular event will occur.

Risk register / log A useful tool to identify, quantify and value the extent of risk and uncertainty relating to a proposal.

Sensitivity analysis Analysis of the effects on an appraisal of varying the projected values of important variables.

Glossary

Shadow price The opportunity cost to society of participating in some form of economic activity. It is applied in circumstances where actual prices cannot be charged, or where prices do not reflect the true scarcity value of a good.

Social Benefit The total increase in the welfare of society from an economic action - the sum of the benefit to the agent performing the action plus the benefit accruing to society as a result of the action.

Social Cost The total cost to society of an economic activity - the sum of the opportunity costs of the resources used by the agent carrying out the activity, plus any additional costs imposed on society from the activity.

Stated preference Willingness to pay for something that is non-marketed, as derived from people's responses to questions about preferences for various combinations of situations and/ or controlled discussion groups.

Substitution The situation in which a firm substitutes one activity for a similar activity (such as recruiting a different job applicant) to take advantage of government assistance.

Switching point or switching value The value of an uncertain cost or benefit at which the best way to proceed would switch, for example from approving to not approving a project, or from including or excluding some extra expenditure to preserve some environmental benefit.

Systematic risk Risk which is correlated with movements in the economic cycle and cannot therefore be diversified away.

Time preference rate Preference for consumption (or other costs or benefits) sooner rather than later, expressed as an annual percentage rate.

Total Economic Value The sum of the use, option and existence value of a good: a term used primarily in environmental economics.

Transfer payment A transfer payment is one for which no good or service is obtained in return.

Uncertainty The condition in which the number of possible outcomes is greater than the number of actual outcomes and it is impossible to attach probabilities to each possible outcome.

Use value Value of something which is non-marketed provided by people's actual use of it. See also Existence value and Option value.

Weighting and Scoring An technique that involves assigning weights to criteria, and then scoring options in terms of how well they perform against those weighted criteria. Weighted scores are then summed, and can then be used to rank options.

Willingness to Accept The amount that someone is willing to receive or accept to give up a good or service.

Willingness to Pay The amount that someone is willing to give up or pay to acquire a good or service.

Glossary

BIBLIOGRAPHY

Andrew B Abel, Avinash K Dixit, Janice C Eberly, Robert S Pindyck (1995), *Options, The Value of Capital and Investment*, (NBER Working Paper 5227), November 1996

Blundell R, Browning M and Meghir C (1984), *Consumer Demand and the Life-Cycle Allocation of Expenditures*, Review of Economic Studies, 61, 1994, 57-80

Boardman, A, Greenberg, D, Vining, A and Weimer, D (1996), *Cost-Benefit Analysis: Concepts and Practice*, Upper Saddle River, N.J. Prentice Hall, 1996

Cowell, F A and Gardiner, K (1999), *Welfare Weights*, (STICERD, London School of Economics, Economics Research Paper 20, Aug 1999

Crafts N (2002), *Britain's Relative Economic Performance 1870 -1999*, Institute of Economic Affairs Research Monograph No. 55, IEA London

Demsetz, H (1969), *Information and Efficiency: Another Viewpoint*, Journal of Law and Economics, Vol 12, pp 1-22

Dixit, A , (2000), *Incentives and Organisations in the Public Sector: An Interpretative Review*, Princeton University

Drury, C (1988), *Management and Cost Accounting*, VNR International, London

Evans, A W (2000), *The Economic Appraisal of Road Traffic Safety Measures in Great Britain*, European Conference of Ministers of Transport. Round Table, Paris

Feldstein, M S (1970), *Choice of Technique in the Public Sector, A Simplification*, The Economic Journal, Dec. 1970

Flyvbjerg, B (2002), *Undersetimating Costs in Public Works Projects*, APA Journal, Summer 2002, Vol. 68, No. 3

Fox, Kennedy and Sugden (1993), *Decision Making – A Management Accounting Perspective*, Butterworth Heinemann in association with CIMA

Franklin D E (2000), *The Morality of Groups*, PhD Thesis, University College London

Gollier, C. (2002), *Time Horizon and the Discount Rate*, IDEI, University of Toulouse, mimeo.

Hart, Shleifer and Vishny (1997), *The Proper Scope of Government: Theory and an Application to Prisons*, Quarterly Journal of Economics, November 1997

Henderson and Bateman (1995), *Hyperbolic Social Discount Rates and the Implications for Intergenerational Discounting*, Environmental and Resource Economics 5: 413-423

House of Commons Public Accounts Committee, *Improving the Delivery of Government IT Projects* (HC65)

Jones-Lee, M W. et al. (1992), *Paternalistic Altruism and the Value of a Statistical Life*, Economic Journal 102 80-90

Jones-Lee, M and Loomes, G (2001), *The Valuation of Health and Safety for Public Sector Decision Making*, Centre for Analysis of Safety Policy and Attitudes to Risk, University of Newcastle upon Tyne

Bibliography

Kula, E. (1987), *Social Interest Rate for Public Sector Appraisal in the United Kingdom, United States and Canada*, Project Appraisal, 2:3, 169–74.

Layard, R (1999), *Appraisal and Evaluation in Human Resource Policies*

Little, I M D and Mirrlees, J A (1994), *The Costs and Benefits of Analysis: Project Appraisal and Planning Twenty Years On*, in R Layard and S Glaister eds Cost Benefit Analysis 2nd ed , Cambridge University Press

Maddison, A. (2001), *The World Economy: a Millennial Perspective*, Paris, OECD.

Newbery, D. (1992), *Long term Discount Rates for the Forest Enterprise*, Department of Applied Economics, Cambridge University, for the UK Forestry Commission, Edinburgh

OXERA (2002), A Social Time Preference Rate for Use in Long-Term Discounting, a report for ODPM, DfT and Defra

Pearce D and Ulph D (1995), *A Social Discount Rate For The United Kingdom*, CSERGE Working Paper No 95-01 School of Environmental Studies University of East Anglia Norwich

Sandmo A (1998), *Redistribution and The Marginal Cost of Public Funds*, Journal of Public Economics 70 365-382

Scott, M.F.G. (1977), *The Test Rate of Discount and Changes in Base Level Income in the United Kingdom*, The Economic Journal, 1989 (June) 219-241.

Scott, M.F.G. (1989), *A New View of Economic Growth*, Clarendon Paperbacks

Smith, C and Flanagan, J (2001), *Making Sense of Public Sector Investment*, Radcliffe Medical Press, Oxford

Vose, D (1996), *Qualitative Risk Anlaysis: A Guide to Monte Carlo Simulation Modelling*, John Wiley & Sons, Chichester

Weitzman M (March 2001), *Gamma Discounting*, American Economic Review, Vol 91, No 1

INDEX

Note: page numbers suffixed 'n' indicate a reference to a footnote.

achievability 9
acquisition and use of property 69–71
'Adding it Up' 7n
additionality 52–4, 101
adjustments 24–6
    for market distortions 21
    for optimism bias 30, 85–6
    for taxes 28
    for variability 88–9
    see also distributional weights; weighting and scoring
adverse selection 52, 101
affordability 9, 19, 39, 101
aggregates 67
agri-environment schemes 65
agricultural land 70
air quality 9, 61, 64–5
amenity values 66, 70
    see also social costs and benefits
anti-discrimination law 94–6
appraisal 3–10
    compared to evaluation 47–8
    definition 2, 101
appraisal period 19
appraisal reports 6
archives 7
assessment, definition 1n, 101
asymmetry of information 52, 101, 102
auditors 7
    see also National Audit Office

base case 5, 5n, 17–36, 101
benefit categories 44
benefit transfer method 21, 65
benefits see costs and benefits
benefits realisation management 44
best option 5, 37–9
bias 4, 28, 29–30, 85–7
    see also optimism bias
biodiversity 66
budget statements 39
building see construction
buildings see construction projects; land and property

cancellation costs 21
capital charges 21
capital costs 85, 101
capital values 69, 71
capital works duration 96
carbon emissions 64n
carbon savings 64
cashflow statements 39
cashflows 19
casualties 61–2
catastrophe risk 97
Centre for Management and Policy Studies (CMPS) 7n, 8, 10
checklist of issues 9–10
choice modelling 57, 57n, 101
climate change effects 64
commercial arrangements 9, 41–2
construction projects 43, 62–3, 87–8
    see also capital works duration; land and property
consultation
    creating options 17
    developing and implementing solutions 5, 37, 40
    risk mitigation 81
    see also specialist advice
consumer focus 10
contingency, definition 101
contingent liabilities 21
contingent ranking and contingent rating 57n, 101
contingent valuation 57, 63, 65, 101
    see also willingness to accept; willingness to pay
contract cancellation costs 21
contract management 9, 44
contractual arrangements for risk mitigation 81
cost-benefit analysis 9
    best option selection 37, 38
    definition 4, 101
    evaluation 45
    land and buildings 77
    recommended technique 4
    see also distributional analysis
cost-effectiveness, land use 72–7
cost-effectiveness analysis
    best option selection 37, 38
    definition 4, 101
    health benefits valuation 60

Index

cost categorisation 20
cost estimation 20–1
    see also plausible estimates
cost of capital, definition 101
cost of retention, vacant land 72
cost of variability in outcomes 88–9, 101
cost utility 60n
costs and benefits 6, 19–26, 59–67
    see also additionality; disamenity impacts; displacement; distributional impacts; employment impacts; environmental impacts; non-market impacts; operating costs and benefits; structural impacts; supply-side impacts; unvalued costs and benefits; valuation
creation of options 5, 17–19
critical success factors 35
crowding out 53, 101

data 4
    see also information
deadweight 53, 54, 101
deaths, prevented 61–2
decision guidelines 37–9
decision to proceed 6, 32, 38, 42
decision trees 31–2
Department for Transport 59, 62
depreciated replacement cost (DRC) 71
depreciation 21
design flexibility 81
design quality 10, 35, 62–3
Design Quality Indicator (DQI) 35
diminishing marginal utility 24, 65, 101
disability discrimination law 94–6
disamenity impacts 67
discount rate 26–7, 97–100, 102
    see also internal rate of return (IRR)
discounted cash flow (DCF), definition 102
discounting 26–8, 56, 101
    see also discount rate
discrimination law 94–6
    see also equality
displacement 53–4, 53n
    definition 53, 102
    regeneration projects 55
disposal of property 72
dissemination of results 7, 47
distance decay 65, 65n
distributional analysis 24–5, 91
distributional impacts 9, 91–6

distributional objectives see equality
distributional weights 24, 92–4
    see also weighting and scoring
do minimum option
    creating options 17
    definition 102
    in large or complex projects 87
    shortlisting 5, 19
do nothing case 47, 53
dual cost analysis 20
dust 67

economic cost see opportunity cost
economic efficiency 51–2, 102
effectiveness
    definition 102
    see also cost-effectiveness
emissions 64–5
employees' time 20, 59–60
employers' time 59
employment impacts
    regeneration projects 55
    see also displacement
environmental impacts 9, 19, 63–7, 70
Environmental Landscape Features (ELF) model 65
equality 9, 11, 24, 52
    see also discrimination law; distributional analysis
equity see equality
equity value of time-savings 59
equivalisation 91–2
estimation
    benefit values 21–2
    costs 20–1
    see also plausible estimates
European Union 10, 56
EuroQol instrument 60
evaluation 4–10, 45–9
    cycle of appraisal and 3
    definition 2, 102
    performance data capture 42, 43
    planning for 2
existence value 88, 102
expected value (EV) 30, 31, 102
externalities 51
externality costs or benefits, definition 102

fatalities, prevented 61–2
financial appraisal, definition 102
financial arrangements 9

financial reporting 44
financial statements 39
fixed costs 20, 32
forests, amenity and recreational values 66
free-riding 51
freehold property 69, 72
full economic cost 20
full time equivalent (FTE) costs 20
funding statements 39

GDP deflator 102
gender discrimination law 94–6
greenhouse gas emissions 64
growth, per capita consumption 97, 98

health and safety 10, 61–2
health benefits 60–1
health issues 10
hedonic pricing 23, 57, 57n, 102
hurdle rates see minimum internal rate of return (IRR)

impact statement, definition 102
impacts see costs and benefits; risks
imperfect information 52
implementation 42–4, 102
inflation 25–6
information 52
    see also data
information asymmetry 52, 101, 102
information management and control 9
injuries 61–2
Integrated Policy Appraisal (IPA) 6, 6n
internal rate of return (IRR) 39, 39n, 102
international development assistance projects 99
intervention, rationale for 4, 11–12, 26, 51–6
irreversibility, definition 103
irreversible decisions 81
irreversible risk 88

justifying action see rationale for intervention

land and property 9, 69–77
    see also construction projects
landscape 65
leakage 53
leasehold property 69, 71, 72
leases and rents 71–2
legislation 9, 56, 94–6
long-term discount rates 98–9, 100

McClements scale 91
management
    of appraisals and evaluations 7
    see also benefits realisation management; contract
        management; information management and control;
        programme and project management; risk
        management
marginal utility
    definition 24, 103
    deriving distributional weights 93–4
    landscape 65
    social time preference rate 97, 98
marital status, discrimination law 94–6
market failure 11, 51, 52, 103
market power 52
    see also monopoly suppliers
market prices see prices
market rents see rents
market value 69, 70, 103
maximin return 38
measurement
    emissions and climate change effects 64–5
    non-market impacts 57–67
    performance 43
    unvalued costs and benefits 34–6
    see also valuation
million tonnes of carbon-dioxide equivalent (MtCO2) 64
minimum internal rate of return (IRR) 39n
minor injuries 62
monitoring 21, 43, 46
monopoly suppliers 21
    see also market power
Monte Carlo analysis 33, 87–8, 103
moral hazard 52, 103
multi criteria analysis see weighting and scoring
multipliers, assessment of additionality 54

National Audit Office 7, 82
net present value (NPV) 26
    adjustment for optimism bias 86
    best option selection 37
    calculation 28
    definition 103
    distributional analysis 91
    internal rate of return (IRR) 39
    property valuation 69
noise 9, 66, 67
non-excludable public goods 51
non-fatal casualties 61–2

Index

non-market impacts 57–67
non-rival public goods 51
non-UK residents and firms 21n
non-working time 59

objectives
    evaluation 46, 47
    regeneration projects 55
    setting 4, 13–15
    see also outcomes
odours 67
Office of Government Commerce (OGC)
    business case templates 7n
    construction project management 43n
    contract management 44
    Gateway review process 8
    procurement options 42
    project management 43
    property disposal 72
    risk management 80, 82
open market value 70, 71
operating costs and benefits 86
opportunity cost
    capital assets 21
    definition 102, 103
    land 72
    valuation of options 19, 20, 21
    valuation of time 20, 59
optimism bias 29–30, 85–7, 103
option appraisal 3, 5, 17–36
    definition 103
    issues 9
    see also adjustments; best option; unvalued costs and
        benefits; valuation
option value 88, 103
outcomes
    cost of variability 88–9, 101
    definition 13
    evaluation 46, 47
    examples 14–15
    regeneration projects 55
    valuation of risks 30
    see also objectives
outputs
    additionality 53–4
    definition 13
    evaluation 46
    examples 14–15
    range of possible 6

outturns see evaluation
over-rented properties 71
own time 59

paired comparisons 57n, 101
partnerships 9, 42, 55
Partnerships UK 42
passing rents 71
pay back period 39, 39n
per capita consumption, growth 97, 98
performance criteria 35
performance management and measurement 43
pilot studies 81
plausible estimates 22, 59–63
pollution see air quality; noise; water quality
precautionary principle 81, 103
predatory pricing 52
present value
    definition 103
    see also net present value (NPV)
presentation of results 6, 47
prevented fatalities and prevented injuries 61–2
price index, definition 103
prices
    adjustment for changes in 25–6
    adjustment for taxes 28
    valuation of costs and benefits 19, 21–2
pricing 27
    see also hedonic pricing; predatory pricing
PRINCE2 43
Private Finance Initiative (PFI) 103
    adjustments for taxation differences 28
    procurement process 42
    risk transfer 41, 84
private sector 37, 40–2, 56, 83–4
procurement 5, 9, 37, 40–2, 81
profit rents 71
programme, definition 1n
programme and project management 37, 42–3
project plans 7
property 62–3, 69–77
proposal, definition 103
public goods 51
Public Private Partnership (PPP) 42, 103
public sector comparator, definition 104
pure time preference 26, 97, 104

quality assurance 7
quality-adjusted life year (QALY) 60

Index

quantification *see* measurement; valuation
quarries 67

racial discrimination law 94–6
rationale for intervention 4, 11–12, 26, 51–6
real option theory, definition 104
real price, definition 104
real terms, definition 104
recreational values 66
redundancy payments 21, 21*n*
regeneration projects 24, 54–6
regional perspectives 10, 94
regulations 8, 9, 42, 56
Regulatory Impact Assessment (RIA) 8
relative price changes 25–6
relative price effect, definition 104
relative prosperity 24, 91–4
relevant cost/benefit, definition 104
rental values 69
rents 71–2
reports 6, 44, 46, 47
required performance criteria 35
required rate of return (RRR) 27, 104
research
    creating options 17
    measuring non-market impacts 58, 59–63
    measuring unvalued costs and benefits 34
    preliminary 4, 11
    valuation of environmental impacts 63–7
    valuation of options 22
residual values 21
resource budgets 19
resource costs 19, 104
resources, definition 104
results, presentation 6, 47
retention of vacant land 72
revealed preference 23, 57, 58
    definition 104
    relative price changes 25
    value of a prevented fatality (VPF) 62
    see also hedonic pricing; willingness to pay
risk, definition 104
risk allocation tables 84
Risk Analysis and Management for Projects (RAMP) 82
risk log *see* risk register
risk management 29, 41–2, 79–82
risk modelling *see* Monte Carlo analysis
risk premium 30
risk register 80, 104

risks 4, 79–89
    best option selection 38
    prevention and mitigation 29, 34, 41, 80–2
    transferring 41, 82–4
    valuation 29, 30–2
    see also catastrophe risk; irreversible risk; Monte Carlo analysis; systematic risk
road schemes, valuation of time 59–60
ROAMEF (Rationale, Objectives, Appraisal, Monitoring, Evaluation, Feedback) cycle 3
rural areas 9

sale of property 72
scenarios 6, 33
scoring *see* weighting and scoring
semi-fixed costs, definition 20
semi-variable costs 20, 32
sensitivity analysis 32–3
    additionality assessment 53
    adjustments for optimism bias 29
    adjustments of operating costs and benefits 86
    cost categorisation 20
    definition 104
    discount rates 99
    estimated benefit values 22
    leases and rents 72
    Monte Carlo analysis inputs 87
    reporting results 6
    residual values 21
shadow price, definition 105
shortlisting options 5, 19
sites *see* land and property
SMART targets 13–14
smells 67
social benefit, definition 105
social cost, definition 105
social costs and benefits 19, 69, 70
    see also amenity values
social time preference rate (STPR) 26, 27, 97–8, 105
solutions, developing and implementing 5, 37–44
specialist advice 7
    Monte Carlo analysis 33
    procurement 42
    property disposal 72
    property valuation 69–70, 71
    relative price changes 26
    valuation of costs and benefits 20, 21
    see also consultation
staff time 20, 59 60

Index

state aids 56
stated preference 23, 57, 57n, 58
    definition 105
    relative price changes 25
    value of a prevented fatality (VPF) 62
    see also willingness to pay
step costs 20, 32
strategic impact of proposals 9
structural impacts 52–3
subsidies 21, 70
substitution, definition 53, 105
summary data 4
summary reports 6, 47
sunk costs 20
supply-side impacts 52–3
switching point or switching value 32, 58, 105
systematic risk, definition 105

targets 4, 13–14, 46
taxes 21, 28
time preference rate 26, 97, 105
time valuation 59–60
total economic value, definition 105
traffic disturbance 67
transfer payment, definition 21n, 105
transferring risk 41, 82–4
transport schemes, valuation of time 59–60

UK Climate Impacts Programme (UKCIP) 64
uncertainty 4, 32–3, 79–89
    definition 105
    long-term discount rates 98
unvalued costs and benefits 22, 34–6, 38
use value, definition 105

vacant land 72
valuation 19–23
    decision to proceed 38
    design quality 62–3
    disamenity impacts 67
    environmental impacts 19, 63–7, 70
    health benefits 60–1
    injuries and casualties 61–2
    land and property 62–3, 69–77
    non-market impacts 57–67
    time 20, 59–60
    see also adjustments; contingent valuation; measurement

valuation adjustments see adjustments
valuation techniques 23
    see also revealed preference; stated preference; willingness to accept; willingness to pay
Value Added Tax (VAT) 28
value of a prevented fatality (VPF) 61–2
variability adjustments 88–9
variable costs 20, 32
visual intrusion 67

waste 9, 67
water quality 9, 65
weighting and scoring 35–6, 38, 58, 58n, 105
    see also distributional weights; expected value
willingness to accept 23, 57–8, 105
    see also contingent valuation
willingness to pay 23, 57–8
    agri-environment schemes 65
    amenity and recreational values of forests 66
    definition 105
    health benefits 60
    prevented fatalities and prevented injuries 61–2, 62n
    see also contingent valuation; revealed preference; stated preference
working time 59
works duration 86